Licensed to Spy

Licensed to Spy

With the Top Secret Military Liaison Mission in East Germany

John A. Fahey

Naval Institute Press
Annapolis, Maryland

Naval Institute Press
291 Wood Road
Annapolis, MD 21402

Library of Congress Cataloging-in-Publication Data
Fahey, John A., 1923–
Licensed to spy : with the top secret Military Liaison Mission in East Germany / John A. Fahey.
p. cm.
Includes index.
ISBN 1-55750-294-3 (alk. paper)
1. United States. Military Liaison Mission—History. 2. Fahey, John A., 1923– 3. Military intelligence—United States—History—20th century. 4. Espionage, American—Germany (East). 5. Soviet Union—Armed Forces—Foreign service—Germany (East). I. Title.
UB271.U5 F34 2002
327.1273047'092—dc21

2001059635

Printed in the United States of America on acid-free paper ♾
09 08 07 06 05 04 03 02 9 8 7 6 5 4 3 2
First printing

To my wife, Barbara, for her loyalty and strong support; to Karen (widow of Maj. Arthur D. Nicholson, killed by a Soviet sentry), who inspires all USMLM members with her wisdom, courage, and understanding; and to the USMLM drivers Mel Ratz, Dick Keezer, Luther Warner, and all the others who put up with my navy mind-set and helped me do my best for my country.

Contents

Licensed to Spy

Prologue

Long before the surrender of Nazi Germany on 9 May 1945, the defeated country's territory was divided into zones and its capital city into sections. A three-power agreement between the United States, Great Britain, and the Soviet Union was reached on 29 June 1944 to establish occupation of zones in Germany and three-power administration of Greater Berlin. On 30 July 1945 a decision was made to designate the cities of Reinickendorf and Wedding as the French sector of Berlin.

In April 1945 American and British armies penetrated deep into what had already been designated as the Soviet Zone of Germany. The two Western armies sat on the west bank of the Elbe River, waiting for the Soviet Army to complete its drive through eastern Germany. Finally Russian army troops arrived to meet the Americans at Torgau on 25 April 1945. The American forces remained in the Soviet Zone until July 1945.

Occupation of Germany as a whole was linked throughout the history of the agreements with the occupation of Berlin. In addition, the withdrawal of American forces from the area west of the Elbe River (approximately one-third of the former German Democratic Republic) for Soviet occupation was directly related to U.S. access to and occupation of West Berlin.

On 15 June 1945 President Harry Truman sent a top secret letter to Stalin in which he proposed a withdrawal of American troops from the Soviet Zone on 21 June, including an understanding concerning the simultaneous entry of national garrisons into Greater Berlin. In his letter Truman remarked also about the agreed-upon allocation of free air, highway, and rail access into Berlin from Frankfurt and Bremen to the U.S. armed forces.

The next day Stalin, in a top secret letter to Truman, confirmed that all agreements made among the victorious powers, including Soviet rights to occupy the portion of East German taken by U.S. troops, depended on U.S. occupation of and access to West Berlin. Stalin asked Truman to delay the withdrawal of American troops from the Soviet Zone until 1 July to accommodate a Soviet victory parade planned for 24 June and also to give time for the Russians to clear mines from all areas of Berlin. Truman agreed.

In 1945 the military occupation of Germany and Berlin by the four powers in their respective zones and sectors was completed. On 5 April 1947 American lieutenant general C. R. Huebner and Soviet colonel general M. S. Malinin signed an agreement that established military liaison missions accredited to the American and Soviet commanders in chief of the occupied zones. The United States Military Liaison Mission (USMLM) to the commander in chief, Group of Soviet Forces–Germany was established in Neu Fahrland, outside Potsdam. The Soviet Military Liaison Mission was established in Frankfurt, West Germany. Similarly, the British and French forces maintained military liaison missions under equivalent agreements signed by British and French commanders and by Soviet general Malinin on 16 September 1946 and 3 September 1947, respectively. Under the provisions of these three agreements, 126 U.S., British, French, and Soviet military personnel were able to travel virtually unimpeded throughout West and East Germany.

Early on the architects of the military liaison missions focused their efforts on cooperation and the coordination of activities related to their zones. As the cold war materialized, the warm feelings of former allies evaporated. The missions realized the magnificent opportunities for intelligence collection by their members who were attached legally to the armies of their potential foes and who were free to travel in their areas of occupation.

The Group of Soviet Forces–Germany stationed twenty-two divisions in the Soviet Zone directly opposite NATO forces stationed in West Germany. Considered the elite vanguard of the Soviet Army, the Soviet forces in East Germany possessed the newest weapons and military equipment. Yet Soviet troop movements could be monitored by British, French, and American personnel. The Soviet order of battle could be confirmed. New Soviet aircraft and ground equipment could be photographed. Military strategies and tactics could be observed on the fields of mock battles. As the aggressive Western intelligence effort in East Germany accelerated, the Soviets enlisted the help of the East German State Security Service—the Staatssicherheitsdienst, or Stasi. The Stasi dealt with political crimes and possessed domestic police powers, including the right to arrest and conduct its own investigations. Its powers were closer to those of the old Russian Cheka than to those of the Nazi Gestapo.

Intelligence collection became a significant part of the mission members' daily tasks. The Stasi's challenge was to stop or harass mission members and to minimize their collection abilities. Both sides became more aggressive as the Berlin crisis approached.

In May 1960 Soviet leader Nikita Khrushchev terminated his relations with U.S. president Dwight Eisenhower when a Soviet missile shot down CIA pilot Francis Gary Powers's high altitude U-2 plane during a reconnaissance flight over the Soviet Union. In early 1961 Khrushchev threatened President John F. Kennedy with unilateral recognition of East Germany, an additional threat to the existence of West Berlin. Military liaison missions increased their concentration on intelligence-gathering activities while liaison activities between the opposing military forces were "placed on the back burner."

Commander John Fahey expected that his assignment as a liaison officer to the American mission would involve interpreter duties and liaison activities only. He did not have the slightest clue that he was about to embark on a mission to collect intelligence. Before reporting for duty in Germany, "spy" was a word far removed from his thoughts. Soon after his arrival he found himself in the middle of the Cold War between the two major world contenders. Reconnaissance and observation were the watchwords. Fahey quickly learned that the Soviet identification card issued to him as an American liaison officer in the Soviet Army was his license to spy.

1

Licensed to Spy

In the dark hours of Sunday, 6 August 1961, a week before the erection of the Berlin Wall, East German border guards stopped my vehicle and snarled, "You're dirty spies!" I was conducting a routine night reconnaissance with a USMLM driver around Berlin in East Germany, close to the West Berlin border. I shouted back in Russian, "Out of the way for a member of the Soviet Army!"

He was right. Although I didn't consider myself dirty, both of us were right. I was attached to the United States Military Liaison Mission to the Group of Soviet Forces–East Germany as an American liaison officer. Liaison activities occupied less than 10 percent of my time; over 90 percent was spent on reconnaissance and spying. If I didn't "bring back the goods," my superiors would quickly haul me out from behind the Iron Curtain. If the Russians caught me too many times, the Soviet Union would declare me persona non grata and require the surrender of my identification card and status as a member of the Soviet forces. I walked a tightrope while facing hundred-mile-an-hour chases, being the target of shootings, and undertaking daring feats to collect intelligence.

It started with a telephone call in May 1959 in Washington, D.C. The Office of Naval Intelligence representative called to inform me that my tour of duty as director of the U.S. Navy Language School was being extended a year to permit the scheduling of my future assignment to Berlin, Germany. Later I learned that the post was not located in Berlin, but in Potsdam, East Germany. I was fluent in Russian and was told to spend some time during the extra year at the school learning enough German to get around easily inside East Germany.

The extra year as director was exciting and challenging. From scratch I had to establish a program for friendly allies to study English, which I later wrote about in my book, *Wasn't I the Lucky One*. In the summer of 1959 two unusual events related to my work at the language school occurred that dominated my attention.

In June Soviet navy captain Nikolai Fedorovich Artamonov, the youngest commanding officer of a destroyer in the history of the Soviet Navy, fled from his base in Poland in a small boat with a young Polish girl. Found in the Baltic Sea by Swedish patrollers, the two defectors were eventually brought to the United States. While they were under CIA protection in a safe house, U.S. navy specialists interrogated Captain Artamonov to learn about Soviet Navy plans, new electronic equipment and weapons, and every other facet of Soviet Navy operations. I received a telephone call informing me that on the following day I would be needed to interpret for a defector from the Soviet Navy.

Knowing that outside the interrogations he might be bored, I decided to buy a present for the man—a model assembly of the USS *Constitution*, "Old Ironsides." Early the next morning a CIA agent in a rented vehicle drove me to a safe house in a farming area somewhere in northern Virginia. I assumed the men I saw scattered around the premises were security personnel. Inside the defector was seated with what appeared to be his girlfriend in a barren room on the first floor. I greeted the Soviet captain with my gift. He eagerly took the box and asked about its contents. He was not familiar with models that could be assembled by hand. The two of us were told to go the basement and wait for the others.

Captain Artamonov began by asking me to call him Nick. I asked him about his background.

"I'm married. This is a picture of my wife and boy in the Soviet Union." He showed me a photo of an attractive young woman and a handsome child. I asked nothing about the young girl upstairs. The captain then told me about his excellent prospects in America. "I have been offered a splendid position as an intelligence specialist at your Naval Observatory. I will be paid seventeen thousand dollars a year."

"I know nothing about you," I said, "but you must be a very important person."

The others arrived. All were navy officers and specialists in weapons, tactics, and the like. They came with photos and drawings from Soviet journals. Nick's reaction to almost every photo or sketch of a new Soviet ship or piece of equipment was, "fantasiya"; to every assumption the interrogators made, "bezuslovno," which in English literally translates to "without condition," meaning "absolutely."

That same routine took place every other day. On off days, when navy lieutenant Bathurst conducted similar sessions with Nick, I listened to a tape of the previous day's session.

On my second day I brought Nick another model, this one of an aircraft carrier. He had finished assembling the ship in two days and was pleased with the finished product. He was surprised that a model of a navy carrier was available in the commercial market.

Every day I had one-on-one chats with Captain Artamonov before the interrogations began. My gut feeling told me he was a double agent. I said nothing about my suspicions to the CIA handlers or to the navy specialists gathered there, but I did make a trip to the Pentagon to express my feelings to a commander in the Office of Naval Intelligence. The commander had been a classmate of mine when we were students in the postgraduate naval intelligence course six years earlier. He agreed with my assessment but informed me that Artamonov had been "swept clean" by the CIA and that no one else in the U.S. Navy had any doubts about his status as a bona fide defector.

Despite my doubts I got along well with Nick. He was intelligent, personable, and likable, and he had a good sense of humor. Many years later, when I was a faculty member at Old Dominion University, a small announcement in the local paper mentioned an appearance by a former Soviet Navy officer, Nicholas Shadrin, at a navy wives' luncheon. I thought, "This must be Captain Nicholas Artamonov! They have given him a new surname but allowed him to keep his first name." I asked one of my Russian language students to attend the luncheon with her mother, who happened to be the wife of a navy captain. I described Nick to Kathy and told her that if he fitted the description, to ask him a series of questions I gave her. Indeed, Shadrin was Captain Artamonov, and Kathy told me that he became flustered when she asked him my questions.

Later the FBI and the CIA used Nicholas Shadrin as a double agent. While on an assignment for these American agencies in Vienna, Shadrin met with high-ranking Soviet intelligence spies on the night of 20 December 1975 and disappeared, never to be seen again in the West. The case has yet to be solved.

A second event that kept me busy at the U.S. Navy Language School while I awaited my assignment to the Soviet Army in East Germany occurred in September 1959, when Nikita Khrushchev visited the United States. The White House wanted a Russian script for a video that had been made of the USS *Nautilus*'s voyage under the North Pole and which President Eisenhower and Khrushchev would be viewing together. I assigned Russian language professor Petrov and Lieutenant Bathurst (an excellent Russian linguist) to the task. Lieutenant Bathurst (speaking Russian) also played the role of a Nautilus seaman in the film.

The White House asked for assistance with another more challenging job related to Khrushchev's visit: furnish Russian linguists to handle communications between Camp David and Moscow. Since faculty members were ruled out, I had to assign students who were themselves undergoing Russian instruction at the school. Although I had chosen the best and most advanced students in our program, none were qualified as interpreters or translators. Yet they accomplished the mission admirably and credited the school with another accolade from the White House.

During the remainder of 1959 and early 1960 little was said about my future assignment to the Soviet Army. I did receive the transcript of a meeting between American and Russian officers when an attempt was made to retrieve a U.S. Army soldier who had defected to East Germany. The effort failed. The American officers involved believed that the soldier had been drugged by the Russians before the arranged confrontation. Later, while on duty at the USMLM, I had an opportunity to meet with the Russians and the defector again in a second attempt to bring him back to West Berlin.

I obtained a copy of my birth certificate with the intention of applying for a passport, but was told that though my family would retain possession of theirs, I could not possess an American passport while on assignment at the USMLM. A Russian identification card would be issued upon my arrival in Berlin. During the entire year of waiting to leave Washington no one hinted at the exciting, audacious, and life-threatening events that lay ahead.

Two days after I arrived in West Berlin I received my Russian photo identification card that labeled me as an American liaison member of the Group of Soviet Forces–Germany. The fine print on the back of the card authorized free access to East Germany from West Berlin, and gave me freedom to travel throughout East Germany. An ominous instruction also noted what to do in case of the passholder's death. My spouse, Barbara, and children were issued Russian identification cards similar to mine, but theirs had no foreboding mention of death.

At the time I did not know that my documents gave me a license to spy. Nor did I know that I would spend most of the next two years in a U.S. Army uniform chasing around East Germany, trying to lose someone tailing me, living in the woods, surreptitiously entering Soviet Army bases and airfields, taking over five thousand photographs of Russian army and air force targets, or spending countless hours in detention rooms trying to convince battle-scarred (and sometimes drunken) Russian officers that I had every right to do what they had caught me doing behind the Iron Curtain. How could I have imagined the exciting and challenging days ahead of me, conducting reconnaissance in East Germany against the Soviet Army and Soviet Air Force? I was an officer in the U.S. Navy.

2

First Negotiations

While waiting to receive my Soviet identification card I spent time scrutinizing the United States Military Liaison Mission's backup operations headquarters in West Berlin. The facility housed a sophisticated photography laboratory (including equipment that could be used for developing ordinary black-and-white photos taken at night without a flash or other lighting), a garage where mission cars were serviced and repaired, and my office in the lower basement (protected by iron bars and a combination lock). A large staff attached to mission headquarters supported the reconnaissance and intelligence collection of the fourteen American passholders authorized to travel throughout the Soviet Zone. My eagerness to get going accelerated.

To begin, the mission chief told me that for my first assignment a driver would take me to the Soviet External Relations Office in Potsdam to retrieve materials wrongly taken from two USMLM reconnaissance officers three weeks before my arrival. German Stasi thugs had broken down the hotel room door of the army officers in the middle of the night, forcibly stripped them of their clothing, and absconded with their cameras, film, maps, and notes. "Don't worry about coming back empty handed," acting chief Lt. Col. Clark Baldwin said. "We have tried twice to retrieve the equipment without success. Soviet colonel Kozlovsky denies knowing anything about the incident. Nonetheless, this meeting will give you a chance to meet the local Russian connection and size up Kozlovsky, Khortov, Zhelanov, and others."

I was intrigued by the opportunity and headed across the border to Potsdam by way of the Glienicke Bridge. Once we arrived at the Soviet building the driver stayed in our vehicle. After a long wait at the door I confronted a glum Soviet junior lieutenant who reluctantly led me into an old-fashioned-looking large room with thick carpets, velvet curtains, windows opening to a brick panorama, and pictures of Marx and Lenin on the wall.

Ten minutes later Russian colonels Kozlovsky and Khortov entered the room and greeted me warmly, like I was a dear old friend. Kozlovsky told me how much he admired the navy, the "best of all armed services." I thanked him and agreed wholeheartedly with his assessment. I added that I was surprised that he, a Soviet Army officer, felt as I did about the navy, especially in view of the Soviet Army's glorious victories against the hated Nazi beasts in World War II.

"Wait a minute," Kozlovsky replied, "I'm talking about your navy, not ours."

"So, you admire my navy and I admire your army. The first, I hope, of many agreements today."

After much small talk I recounted the details of the hotel incident (as far as I knew them) and asked for the return of the material forcibly taken from the U.S. officers. Kozlovsky denied any knowledge of the event. I turned the discussion back to World War II, especially to the turning point of the war at Stalingrad and the friendly meeting of the Americans and Russians at Torgau, on the banks of the Elbe River. About an hour into our dialogue Kozlovsky suddenly changed the subject and said, "As a token of our personal friendship, I will give you the cameras, but only the cameras."

The abrupt turnaround in the discussion shocked me. I decided not to push my luck by demanding the maps, film, and notes, though Kozlovsky's offer was an open admission that the German Stasi and the Soviet Army were in cahoots. After we said our warm good-byes I left with two cameras and several telephoto lenses. I expected an ungrateful response for not getting more out of Kozlovsky, but back at headquarters Lieutenant Colonel Baldwin was pleased and happy with my booty.

Baldwin then had a second liaison assignment for me. He wanted me to go with him to confront the Russians again about a U.S. Army soldier who had supposedly defected to the East Germans. An earlier attempt to get him back had failed. The soldier's father had written to his congressman for a second time, who in turn put pressure on the U.S. Army to force another confrontation with the Russians. The father had received a second letter from his son, who wrote, "The cigarettes over here taste like horseshit!" The boy's father said that it was obvious that his son wanted to return.

I recalled that this same soldier was the subject of the transcript of a meeting between American and Soviet officers that I had read while still in Washington. The U.S. Military Liaison Mission officer who interviewed the young man felt that the Russians had drugged him. At the same time he also believed that this defector did not want to come back to the West.

Acting mission chief Baldwin arranged a night meeting with the Russians to discuss the defector. In the same room where Kozlovsky had given me the cameras we encountered four Russian officers and the soldier. The Russians allowed us to question him without interference of any kind. The soldier, who was in his early twenties, seemed unwilling to answer. He was lethargic, distant, and not at all enthused by our presence. The only hopeful signs came from the Russians, who urged us to continue what was turning out to be a one-way conversation with the soldier. Finally it dawned on me: they wanted to get rid of him. I said, "You want us to take him out of here."

"We wanted him to leave months ago when your army officers came to get him. He's a pain in the ass!"

I asked the soldier if he would like a cigarette. He brightened up for the first time when I gave him an American cigarette. I told him that we could take him back, but he must realize that he would face disciplinary action in the West. "I don't care," he replied. "At least the cigarettes don't taste like horseshit."

Once alone with us on the way back to the border, the soldier didn't stop talking. He thought the meetings with mission representatives were part of a Russian trick to take him away and terminate him. In this case everyone was a winner: the Russians were happy to get him off their hands, the congressman would be given more time to serve his other constituents, the U.S. Army would get a break from congressional pressure, and, most important, the soldier could smoke again with pleasure. The mission credited me with another coup. Clark thought the cigarette offer had done the trick.

"What a fabulous assignment!" I thought. "This duty is going to be great fun." In my exhilaration, however, I couldn't anticipate the scary days and nights ahead of me, a naval officer with a license to spy. Nor could I see the appearance of the new mission chief, who was no Clark Baldwin.

3

Orientation Trips

In May 1960 I began conducting operational tours throughout the Soviet Zone. During the orientation period and initial reconnaissance tours I rode with a U.S. Army officer and a driver. As a commander in the U.S. Navy I outranked all the mission members except the deputy and the chief. If we were detained by the Russians for entering into a restricted area or military complex, or detained for any other reason, as senior officer on the tour it was my responsibility to negotiate with the Russians for our release. At the beginning, though, junior army officers were in charge. I learned quickly that those junior army officers could quickly place us in jeopardy.

The military mission's terminology for detention was "clobbered." If caught by the Soviets or East Germans, the senior American officer on the reconnaissance trip had to rely on his cunning and wisdom to talk their way out of the situation.

Capt. Leo Geleta headed up my first orientation trip. Geleta's main interest when we found ourselves outside of our assigned target area was to collect anything left behind by the Russians after they had ended their training exercises. Before leaving wooded areas the Soviet military typically cleaned up all but what the troops had used for toilet paper. (It is well known that at the ballet in Moscow's Bolshoi Theater, the Soviet newspaper,

Pravda, was the only thing available for toilet paper. The Soviet Army didn't fare any better: the defense newspaper, *Krasnaya Zvezda*, and letters from home were the only wiping substances available when the Soviet Army operated in the field.)

Captain Geleta's modus operandi was to instruct the driver to follow the narrow trails among trees in the woods, while the two officers walked on each side of the vehicle searching for discarded human waste. Leo considered items in the Soviet defense newspaper and letters from home to Soviet soldiers to be extremely valuable intelligence, providing Soviet secrets and indications of troop morale. When the Soviet Army exited training areas, the soldiers often left newspaper and personal mail toilet paper.

As we entered the woods it was obvious that the enlisted driver was happy to be driving the car. It wasn't long before we encountered litter at the side of the trails, all of which had been used as toilet paper. Though neither of us had gloves, Captain Geleta was unconcerned and eagerly stuffed his spoils into the vehicle's trunk. When the trunk was full he began to throw the soiled paper into the back seat where I was to sit during the remainder of the two-day tour.

The walk in the woods was an eerie and precarious situation. We knew that the silence would be broken only by the crack of a Soviet sentry's rifle if we were spotted and, the deeper we penetrated into the forest, the more difficult it would be for us to exit if discovered. I wondered whether this collection effort was worth the risk.

If I found a particularly nasty clump, I called it to Leo's attention in order to avoid any more contact than necessary with the foul prize. Leo would gladly rush to my side, taking great delight in the size of the find. Two hours later Captain Geleta was satisfied with the quantity of his treasures. The back seat of our vehicle was half full, leaving just enough room for me to join the spoils.

"Next time, Captain, if we have to do this, please wait until the end of the tour to begin the collection," I begged. I suddenly felt the glamour and wonder of USMLM duty behind the Iron Curtain fading away. Having to sit beside a pile of human excretion for two days was to me far beyond the call of duty. One irony of our treks through the woods became apparent later when I returned to the United States and began receiving issues of *Krasnaya Zvezda*, which were sent to me directly by air mail from Moscow. As the back issues accumulated in my home, Barbara would often complain about the odd fishy smell of the mailed copies. To me, however, the newspapers' odor was a welcomed sweet contrast to the issues I remember being used as the only toilet paper available to the Soviet Army on maneuvers in East Germany.

Once we returned to Potsdam after this first orientation trip I grumbled to Leo about the nature of the collection effort. Leo responded that "intelligence is a dirty business."

My second orientation tour was guided by Captain R., and again I was in the back seat. As we crossed the Glienicke Bridge from West Berlin into Potsdam we sighted a black Mercedes 300 parked on the Soviet side of the Havel River.

Captain R. turned around to me and said, "Good, we got tails."

"What," I wondered, "could be good about this?"

The Mercedes followed at a distance of about fifteen yards from our back bumper. I asked where we were going. "We will take them into the forest on the dirt roads and lose them in the dust."

The month was June and the fields and roads had been dry since April. We led the Mercedes into the woods by a dusty dirt road. The driver stepped on the gas and we took off at more than sixty miles per hour, leaving a cloud of dust that obliterated the tail car. We turned right onto a cross road and then made a second right. The back seat had no seat belt and I was bouncing around like a rubber ball. A third right turn got us back onto the asphalt road, where the driver sped up to ninety miles per hour. I looked back. As we turned into the woods a second time the tail car was just turning onto the asphalt road. During this second race through the forest we stayed longer, made several more turns, and churned billowing dust behind us that reached the top of the trees. Then once again we were on the asphalt road. Looking back I sighted the Mercedes in the far distance.

"In we go again!" Captain R. shouted. The dust was just beginning to settle as we sped around in the woods for the third time. When we came out again there was no sign of the tail.

"That's how to lose them in the late spring and summer," the captain boasted.

When I began to feel nauseous during the first chase through the woods, I decided we needed to find a different way to lose a tail.

My next surprise was our violation of a warning sign that prohibited passage by mission members into an area. A Soviet guard on sentry duty was standing at the top of a hay wagon parked near the sign. He held a rifle in one hand and a red flag in the other. A young girl was sitting beside him. As we sped past the sign I expected a crack of rifle fire and a bullet to come crashing through the rear window. I threw myself onto the floor. The only sound I heard was laughter.

"Look back," R. said. I crawled up from the car floor, looked out the rear window, and saw the Soviet sentry waving the red flag. "They never shoot," R. added.

The driver was still laughing, and Captain R. joined in.

We found nothing in the restricted area and little of consequence during that entire reconnaissance tour. On my first orientation tour I rode with human excretion. On the second I was thrown from side to side in the back seat and then humiliated by a driver and junior officer for ducking an expected bullet. As badly as I felt, I knew I wasn't alone in my misery: there were two chagrined and angry Stasi officers with a prized Mercedes covered in dirt and dust, and a Soviet soldier who had failed his assignment. We were unarmed and directed to lose tails who were armed and who had orders to stop us, just as all Soviet military personnel were supposed to do. Would they always hesitate to shoot? Is there a better way to lose a tail or to enter a restricted area? It wasn't long before I found the answers to these questions.

4

The Art of Losing Tails

Orientation tours were over. The plan for my maiden voyage as a reconnaissance tour officer was a trip through East Germany, sure to keep me out of trouble. No major Soviet installations lay near the secondary roads or small towns on the route. The USMLM operations officer assigned the mission's best driver, Sgt. Dick Keezer, to travel with me on what was sure to be a safe, uneventful trip.

USMLM drivers lived at the mission's villa in Neu Fahrland in the Soviet Zone outside Potsdam. I instructed Keezer to leave the Potsdam mission house early in the morning, drive to the West Berlin USMLM headquarters to get my equipment, cameras, and maps, and then pick me up at 5:00 A.M. at my West Berlin home.

Keezer arrived on time. He mentioned that he had seen Major Warren and his air force driver at Berlin headquarters. Warren had asked Keezer if any tails were positioned on the Potsdam side of the Glienicke Bridge. Keezer had seen one Mercedes waiting on the East German side.

We passed the Berlin golf course on our way through West Berlin to the bridge that crossed into the Soviet Zone when Keezer suddenly said, "That's odd. There is someone at the edge of the golf course, looking in our direction with binoculars."

Immediately I said, "Take a right at the next road."

"What's up?"

"You told Major Warren that there was one tail car waiting on the East German side. Well, that's Warren and his driver on the golf course waiting for us to pass by and cross the bridge first. The Stasi tail will follow us and Warren will go scot-free."

"Great, Commander. We'll wait and let them take the tail."

We parked and had waited about twenty seconds when I changed my mind. "Let's go. This is just a familiarization trip. Warren's on an air force intelligence mission. We'll take the tails."

None of the USMLM drivers relished the high speed chases necessary to lose tails. It was nerve-racking and dangerous.

"You've outfoxed Major Warren. Don't do it, Commander."

"Hurry up. Let's go! Warren will start for the bridge in a few minutes." Keezer frowned, obviously unhappy with me.

Sure enough. The tail car waiting on the Communist side began following us as soon as we cleared the Soviet checkpoint. We drove to the autobahn that encircled the city with the tail car fifty feet behind us. I didn't have the slightest idea how to lose the two German Stasi agents.

We traveled about three miles down the autobahn when we saw a French mission car traveling in the opposite direction, toward Potsdam. Once the French air force officers saw the tails behind us they immediately veered off and crossed the autobahn island. The car sped up and caught the tail car, then squeezed into the small space between us.

"Dick, floor it!"

The order was not needed. Keezer already was exceeding seventy miles per hour.

"Get in front of that large truck. Stay close to his front bumper, then exit at the off-ramp about half a mile ahead."

My last view of the Mercedes before we pulled in front of the truck was of the Stasi thugs finally passing the French vehicle. The French had slowed them, but they were beginning to close the gap. We flew off the autobahn, turned left at the top of the exit, and stopped to look down from the overpass.

The Mercedes sped past the off-ramp, still well behind the truck. As the tail car approached the overpass we could see two faces looking up at us. We proceeded across the overpass to a maze of secondary roads. The remainder of the trip (minus the tails) was pleasant and uneventful, as expected.

Keezer was delighted with the trip's outcome, and gleefully anticipated giving Major Warren and his driver a ribbing about how we had taken the tails in order to set them free. I asked Keezer to let Major Warren believe that he had outwitted us. Keezer promised me that he would not reveal our actions even if the air force driver brought up the matter.

I said nothing to Major Warren, who ultimately became a good friend. I learned an important lesson that day, one that would help me in future intelligence work: trust no one, friend or foe. I also learned that it is possible to lose a tail without resorting to a one-hundred-mile-per-hour chase in the woods.

Maneuvering a 1957 Chevrolet against a Mercedes driven by armed young Stasi officers doesn't appear to offer fair odds. Yet it wasn't long before I realized that we had the advantage. Our USMLM 1957 Chevrolets were brand-new, even in the 1960s. They sported some primitive early "James Bond" devices and modifications, including a switch to turn off the rear brake lights (handy for making a turn in the darkness), extra heavy duty shock absorbers, and a forty-gallon gas tank.

We possessed some psychological benefits on our side as well. The East Germans treasured their West German Mercedes cars. They continually inspected and removed every speck of dust or dirt from the hood. When it came time to take a chase through muck and mire, they sometimes abandoned the pursuit. Their behavior often reflected the humorous Berlin description of a German male's order of preference: "First is the dog, then the car, followed by the children, and last the Frau."

Another advantage was the orders we had to lose tails. No doubt the Stasi agents had instructions not to lose us, but I learned that when we did lose them, the Stasi fabricated the remainder of the trip scenario and submitted a false report to their superiors. During over two years of duty at the USMLM I never heard of a mission officer failing to lose a German tail.

Since I was only in my thirties I had great bladder control, which was a blessing in aggravating and shaking chases. The Germans tried to match our extra gasoline capacity with portable jerry cans. If I stopped my vehicle after a prolonged nonstop trip, the East Germans would run to the trees to relieve themselves before refilling their car tanks from their cans. Halfway through their private business I would take off. If they chanced to catch me I would run them until their car was out of gas. If they filled their tanks from the cans while my driver and I sought relief, we would dash off before the tails had the same opportunity. Their bladders never held out. No one in our mission cared about how long we were gone on assignments. Completing an assignment could always wait until we lost the German agents. We presented the tails with the impossible choice of bladder relief or gas replenishment—a foolproof tactic for losing a tail.

During the wet season if the tails ventured onto muddy trails after us, invariably their vehicles got stuck in the mud. If my Chevrolet became struck, the driver and I would use the nearest tree trunk and winch the vehicle to higher ground. Under such circumstances the tails would admit defeat. Although the Stasi agents were armed they didn't shoot. Strangely, this "mud method" was considered losing a tail fair and square. It was always wise to keep within a few hundred feet of a tree to be able to winch our vehicle from the mud. As part of the unwritten rules of the game, I learned that if I was being followed I should not drive willy-nilly across fields—we were to stay on a road or trail or invariably they would brandish their weapons.

During the winter it was possible to lose tails in the snow because the Stasi would slowly fall behind. Once out of their sight I was able to make several turns onto other roads, shaking them for the rest of the trip.

Once I was ordered to stay all night inside an area between Berlin and the northern coast of East Germany. At daybreak I planned to conduct reconnaissance along the northern area of the Soviet Zone. I left Potsdam with a tail. To the chagrin of my driver, I made him drive due north at no more than ten miles per hour all night. It kept me in the area all night and greatly aggravated the tails. At daylight we reached the city of Stralsund. The Mercedes behind us had steam billowing from its engine and finally broke down. We continued our assignment alone. Months later one of the Stasi agents defected and brought to the West copies of some tails' reports. I was surprised to read an account of this trip. The report indicated that the agents had tailed me during the entire reconnaissance tour, writing that I had collected sand samples from a beach, which was not true.

If we ate our lunch in the woods before losing a tail, the German agents following us would eat theirs while positioned several yards away from us. Normally we never exchanged a single word. However, on one of his first trips with me Maj. Bill Schneider learned that among ourselves we referred to one of the tails as "Gummy Kopf." Once during lunch Schneider hollered what was meant to be a pleasantry to this Stasi agent, calling him "Mr. Gummy Kopf." I was caught off guard by Schneider's action and had no idea that he didn't know that "Gummy Kopf" was not the tail's name, but in English roughly translates as "rubber head." The agent made an angry retort as he was being restrained by his colleague. From then on that agent was one of the most difficult tails to lose and I was always relieved when "Mr. Gummy Kopf" was not behind me.

During more than two years at the USMLM I had a verbal exchange with tails on only two occasions. The first was on a trip to the vicinity of the city of Karl-Marx Stadt in the south. The trip involved a large, temporarily restricted area that crossed East Germany below Berlin, leaving only a narrow strip open at the far west side of the country. It would have taken eight to ten hours to circumvent the forbidden area to get to the city of Karl-Marx Stadt. The following day I was expected to cover a line west of Karl-Marx Stadt, via the cities of Gera, Jena, Erfurt, and Gortha, on to Eisenach in order to count Soviet military units proceeding north into the restricted area.

I left Potsdam with a tail and did not have the time to lose it before nightfall. I decided to head due south directly toward the restricted area boundary. The German agents were getting extremely nervous as I approached the area's boundary, blowing their horn and pulling alongside our vehicle. When we were only one mile from the forbidden area I directed my driver to stop. The tail car stopped behind us.

In all my encounters with Russians I spoke Russian with ease, but my German was clumsy. I walked to the Stasi car door and said, "You have a choice. Let us go through the restricted area directly to Karl-Marx Stadt or we both drive ten more hours around the temporarily restricted area."

"Why should we?"

"Because we will arrive at a nice hotel in Karl-Marx Stadt by 6:00 P.M."

"What hotel?"

"I forget the name. The one with a band and dancing."

"Go through! No turns!"

"Thanks!"

We arrived at the Karl-Marx Stadt hotel at 6:00 P.M., showered, changed clothes, and entered the dining room at 7:15. The German Stasi agents, seated near the door, were already eating and drinking beer when we entered the room. At 8:00 the dancing began. The two tails each chose blonde beauties as their dancing partners. After the first dance they brought the girls back to their table. During the next hour the Germans continued to dance and drink and paid less and less attention to us.

I told my driver to get ready to sneak out of the dining room at 9:45.

"Get our bags and all the gear to the car. Park the car at the lot's exit and then come back to the table."

The driver returned about 10:00. We followed the agents' movements carefully. Finally, when both were out of sight on the dance floor, we quietly left the room, raced across the parking lot, and were gone.

We covered the assigned territory all night and all the next day. At dusk we checked in at the Wartburg, a hotel near Eisenach that was attached to the famous Wartburg Castle, where Martin Luther had translated the Bible. We dined in the elegant hotel restaurant. An orchestra dressed in tuxedos played light music. We were not only without the presence of the hated German agents, but no other diners appeared during the entire evening. The next morning we learned that we were the hotel's only guests.

We awoke to see a winter wonderland. It had snowed all night. After a leisurely breakfast we packed our bags. The USMLM vehicle, parked far below at the bottom of a steep hill, now had a German tail car parked behind it. When we arrived at the car I noticed that the two agents were not the ones that we had left drinking and dancing in Karl-Marx Stadt. These two new agents must have been sent from Berlin and had driven all night to get to Eisenach.

Contrary to the practice of other USMLM officers, I did not believe in losing tails on the way home after a mission had been completed. However, on this occasion we did lose them, only because they couldn't keep up with us in the snow. Why lose a tail after a mission has been completed? It seemed to me a matter of personal pride for others to always shake tails no matter the circumstances. Many army officers who rode with me were disturbed about my refusal to lose a tail on the way home to Potsdam.

On returning from one reconnaissance tour a certain Major M. ordered the driver to stop our car in a spot that placed the car tailing us on the railroad tracks, just as an express train approached. The gatekeeper kept open the gate in front of us but had closed the gate behind the tail car, trapping the Germans on the track. I countered M.'s order to stop. I was thankful that the army driver recognized rank over branch of service and moved the car forward. It was a close call for the tail car. The major was furious that I had countermanded his order. Even the gatekeeper in the tower was unhappy that we let the tails escape. Not aware that I had probably saved their lives, the two Germans in the tail car vented their fury at me with all sorts of gestures.

Like the other mission officers, I never failed to lose tails when I departed on a reconnaissance tour, but when they began following me at a final hotel stay at the end of my mission I usually let them follow me home. When I lost them at the beginning of a tour it was always fair and square. Toward the end of my assignment at the USMLM, the German agents did fire their weapons at me once when the army captain driving our car drove directly toward a member of the surveillance team before I could stop him. The incident happened on the way home. (The consequences of this shooting episode are described in a later chapter.)

The mind-set of most army officers within the USMLM—that the Stasi hoods, the Vopos (people's police), the Grepos (border police), the Trapos (transportation police), and the Russian military forces were all "the enemy"—diminished my fellow officers' effectiveness as spies. I found it a wise practice for everyone on both sides to do their jobs. Our mission was to conduct intelligence observation and collection. Their mission was to stop us. An unemotional approach seemed to me to be the best characteristic for an overt spy to have. On occasion, when situations got out of hand, the Stasi shot to kill. In my case the agents shot over my head. I believe that my reluctance to deliberately harass them, as well as my use of more subtle methods to lose them, resulted in less anger on their part and provided better opportunities for collecting intelligence on my part.

5

Detentions

During my two years as a mission officer I certainly suffered the most from my detentions in the Soviet Zone. "Suffered" is probably not the best description, because many arrests turned out to be enjoyable experiences (though others were not). On my first reconnaissance trips I did not know how far to penetrate into military areas or how dangerous it was to stay in one sensitive area for longer than twenty minutes. As a result I was detained seven times during my first six tours. I concluded my tour of duty at the USMLM by "earning" more detentions than any other mission officer, but after those first detentions the others were spread out over the entire tour of duty.

Although we were granted freedom to travel as American liaison officers attached to the Group of Soviet Forces–Germany, we were forbidden to be in restricted areas, military units, factories, or other similar enterprises. To collect intelligence, however, we regularly had to enter restricted military areas. I was never caught inside a Soviet airfield or a missile base, only because I managed to escape before being detained. But if a USMLM officer was sighted inside a base, it was not unusual for the Soviets to block every road in a circumference of about ten kilometers from the base. Detentions conducted by the Germans were often initiated at the spot of the alleged violation.

After an arrest the local Russians or Germans would telephone the kommandant of the military district. The kommandant, usually a Soviet colonel, would appear at the scene and escort the offenders to a detention room at his headquarters for a stay of hours or days, depending on the whim of the kommandant or the seriousness of the offense. With over half a million Soviet and East German soldiers in a territory smaller than Tennessee (East Germany), it took stealth and shrewd thinking to avoid detention.

Detentions that resulted from making foolish mistakes or for no good cause were particularly annoying. Once our driver had misread a detour sign in Freiberg (a city of no consequence) and turned into a very short cul de sac. We passed a huge brick building surrounded by a ten-foot brick wall, then turned around to leave. As we passed by the building the second time two German soldiers armed with AK-47s blocked our path. We stopped. I got out of the car. One of the soldiers pushed me against the brick wall with his machine gun. The other German aimed his gun at the army officer and the driver in the car. The soldier guarding me kept the machine gun pointed at my stomach for the next four hours.

Finally a Russian colonel arrived at the site. He stepped out of his vehicle and passed through the wall's entrance into the German kaserne without giving me a glance. After thirty minutes he returned and told me I could leave. The German soldier removed the gun. The Russian colonel turned away quickly and wasted no time in getting to his vehicle.

I ran to him and said angrily, "I don't appreciate you passing by me when I was held at gunpoint."

"So, you were on forbidden military territory. What do you expect?"

"We are on a public street and this looks like a fish factory."

The colonel began to laugh. "A fish factory?" He stared at the red building and shouted, "It does! You're right! A fish factory!"

I had seen Russians laugh and cry at the drop of a hat, but I had never seen one so amused by the appearance of a building. When he recovered his senses, the colonel told me again that we could leave. Although I was no longer being guarded, the other German soldier kept his machine gun pointed at the occupants of the mission car. The colonel entered his vehicle, and I just barely was able to stop him from leaving. He jumped out of the vehicle when I explained that the second German soldier refused to move.

The colonel approached the soldier and in Russian told him to return to the building. The soldier refused to budge. The Russian officer became furious and three times ordered the soldier to leave without getting a response. The colonel was stamping his feet when we heard other Germans, unseen from behind the wall, shouting, "Raus! Raus!" Then both soldiers departed.

The Russian colonel's face was still red from the encounter. I said, "You get angry about the Germans failing to obey your orders. How do you think I felt against a wall for four hours with an AK-47 pushed into my belly?"

The Russian began to mellow and laughed. "And worst of all, at a fish factory." The colonel then departed, saying, "I'll see you."

"Not unless I see you first, Colonel."

It was an uncomfortable detention, but at least it lasted only half a day and took place in the fresh open air. Most detentions were conducted in a windowless room with a peculiar, stuffy odor that seemed to exist in all Soviet military buildings.

After only three months as an overt reconnaissance spy I still hadn't learned how to gather intelligence information without getting caught. I could lose a tail without much difficulty, but always pushed my luck in my zeal to bring back valuable information. I lacked the patience to work my way slowly into a sensitive area and often suffered the consequences.

I knew that if I got too many detentions I would be transferred out of the USMLM. Just when I seemed to be getting the hang of it, Capt. Mike Gleason earned a temporary pass to the Soviet Zone as a reward for his diligent work at the USMLM operations section in West Berlin. Captain Gleason had firsthand information of all of the intelligence targets in East Germany, and craved the opportunity to see and photograph them for himself. His tour of duty at the USMLM was almost over though he had never had an opportunity to travel behind the Iron Curtain.

None of the tour officers seemed willing to take Mike on a trip. He spoke neither Russian nor German and couldn't go alone (that is, with a driver but no other USMLM officers). I agreed to let him accompany me on a long trip, first to the south of Berlin and then to the northern coast of the country. Early in the morning of 17 August 1960 we left Potsdam.

While traveling south of Leipzig near the city of Rotha, we decided to take a one-lane winding road to the top of a high hill in order to photograph a cluster of antennas. The hilltop resembled the apex of a triangle. As we reached the hill's summit I directed the driver to position the vehicle facing down the steep hill. Mike and I walked about fifty yards through the brush to reach the towering mast of the antenna array, then prowled around the building at the base of the antennas. A light burned inside but there was no sign of life. We proceeded to take photos for about fifteen minutes, using a number of different lenses on my cameras.

When I began to feel uneasy, I motioned for Mike to follow me back to the car, though when I reached the car I discovered that he was not behind me. I retraced my steps and found him back at the antennas, still photographing. I ordered him to return to the car. This time he followed me closely. When we reached the edge of the bushes, about twenty feet from the vehicle, we were shocked to see an East German vopo standing three feet directly behind the car. We split up, one of us creeping to the left and the other to the right. Just when we were nearly abreast of the vopo our driver saw the policeman for the first time and shouted something unintelligible at the top of his lungs. Mike and I dove for the rear doors. The driver needed no orders and sped down the hill. We heard no shots.

Fortunately no vehicle was coming up the one-lane road. We reached the main highway to Leipzig and after traveling a couple of miles further on we turned into a wooded area. Relieved, all three of us laughed about the vopo who was apparently puzzled about our presence at the site and too confused to shoot. Though all USMLM vehicles and persons were supposed to possess diplomatic immunity, I decided that we should hide in the trunk all the film we had taken of the site. We ate a snack in the pleasant surroundings, then headed to Leipzig.

As we approached the environs of the city we saw five German police vehicles blocking the road ahead of us. We all naively wondered what had happened but soon found out when the officers aimed their weapons at us. We were ordered at gunpoint to follow them, convoy style. I refused, telling the vopo in charge that I was driving directly to the Soviet kommandant in Leipzig to report this violation of our right to travel freely in the Soviet Zone.

At the kommandant's headquarters Mike and I were immediately arrested and placed in a detention room. We waited only ten minutes before being ushered into a large map room. On a drafting table sat a large map of the area, with outlines of restricted areas. Two Soviets (a colonel and a major) began charging us with a serious violation as a result of our presence on a hill within a restricted area. Not admitting that we had been in the area, I pointed out that there certainly was a question as to whether a location so close to the marked restricted border would be considered in or out, especially because of the width of the line drawn on the Russian map.

The major then began the interrogation: "Regardless, admit you were there."

"I will not admit to anything."

"You were seen!"

"Not by a Russian."

"I'm not saying who saw you."

"We saw Russians all the way to Leipzig. You cannot bring one Russian who will say we were there."

"This is true. We can't."

"Germans are always saying bad things about us and about you, too. We don't recognize that they have any authority in the Soviet Zone. That's why I drove straight to your headquarters when they stopped me at the entrance to your city."

The major turned to the Russian colonel. "Comrade Colonel Smirnov, Lieutenant Colonel Fahey does not believe that he was in a restricted area."

Smirnov replied, "He was seen."

"Not by any of our fellows."

Smirnov turned to me. "You speak Russian like us. Have you read our literature?"

"Sure, Alexander Sergeevich Pushkin is my favorite."

Smirnov brightened. "Mine too. Pushkin hated the tsar."

"But not as much, Colonel, as Tsar Nicholas hated Pushkin."

Small talk continued for another five minutes before Mike and I were released. When we returned to our car the German vopos were still surrounding it and the driver inside. The Russian major escorted us to the car, shook hands warmly, and wished us well. The vopos shouted angrily as we headed north out of the center of the city. The brief detention was over, but it was the seventeenth of August and more excitement was still ahead.

We continued our reconnaissance tour by heading north to the coast. On our way Mike pleaded for a look at the Altengrabow training area. To my knowledge no American had ever driven through this Soviet military training area, which covered a stretch of about twenty miles running south of the Helmstedt–Berlin autobahn. The map of the area contained a number of villages, including Altengrabow.

We entered the area via a dirt road that soon deteriorated into a muddy "roller coaster" ride. Our driver had great difficulty steering the car through the ruts and deep depressions that had been made by Soviet tanks. At first Mike enjoyed the ride and relished taking photographs of the Soviet Army equipment he sighted near the road. Soon our vehicle was completely covered with mud. The only view available was a blurry one through the front windows, which were barely kept clear by the windshield wipers. There were no villages, no sign of humanity, only mud, ditches, and deep ruts. Mile after mile we struggled on at a turtle's pace. After two long hours a parade ground with four platoon-sized formations came into view.

I told the driver to stop the car. I got into the driver's seat and drove the car into the widest space I could find between the military formations. No one on the field moved. I sighted a Russian officer ahead, rolled the muddy driver's window down, and drove the vehicle abreast of him.

"Comrade Colonel, request your permission to proceed to the hard surface road ahead."

Looking puzzled, he replied, "Granted."

I drove slowly, straight out of the military complex onto the asphalt highway a mile from the training area. Had we been caught inside the training area, a detention of twelve hours would have been the minimum expected punishment. Mike laughed, hardly able to say, "They had no idea who we were!"

"You see, Mike, how easy it is to bluff your way out of a situation without racing across the zone."

I had had enough of the Soviet Army for one day. After stopping for a car wash we headed for the coast.

It was late in the afternoon when we arrived in Rostock. During an earlier trip to Rostock I had been tempted to take the ferry across to Breitling. The ferry route passed close by the naval shipyard in Rostock (which offered an excellent opportunity for photographing ships undergoing repair), but the route also terminated in a restricted area. While it was no great problem to enter restricted zones in rural or wooded areas, entering one from a city or congested area was risky. When we arrived at the ferry, a German was loading the cars. He did not pay any attention to us until our front wheels passed the ramp onto the ferry, when he blocked our progress and ordered us to back up. I refused to comply.

Soon the ferry operator appeared, shouting in German, "Back off!"

In the distance I could see several Soviet Navy ships in the shipyard. There was no way that I was going to back the car's front wheels off that ferry.

I stayed in the car and hollered, "No!"

The exchange, "Back!," "No!," continued for about five minutes. Just when I thought that vopos might appear, the ferry operator caved in. "Go forward!"

Strangely, once on the ferry no one said a single word to any of us. I exited our vehicle and, using a Leica camera and two telephoto lenses, photographed every vessel on the waterfront of the shipyard. I was pleased to find three Soviet Navy ships among several German cargo vessels.

I knew that once we left the ferry we would have to leave the restricted area by road and come out from behind a sign that stated that entry into the area was forbidden to members of foreign liaison missions. While on our way in we had passed a German naval installation along a major road and had to return by it a second time. On the second pass by it the road in front of the installation was blocked by five German sailors with machine guns. They held us on the road for an hour before the Soviet kommandant from the Rostock district arrived.

During our wait one of the German sailors came to my car window and said, "How much time do you think you will get for this espionage?"

I did not respond.

"Do you think that you will get ten years like your spy, Gary Powers?"

"Gary Powers got ten years?"

"Yes. This morning. Remember this date, August 17, 1960. You also will be severely punished."

"Maybe. Maybe not. Of one thing I am sure."

"What?"

"That you know the punishment of Gary Powers, but after we leave, you'll never know what happened to us."

"I do know that it will be harsh."

Soviet colonel Saigada arrived and escorted us to his headquarters in Rostock. I had met him two weeks earlier. Inside his detention room Saigada conducted the interrogation. "This is no joke! You drove past a restricted sign into a forbidden area."

"Who saw me?"

"You were seen."

"By whom? He or she? Where? Someone is lying to you."

"You were seen driving by the sign."

"Colonel, no one saw me pass by a sign into the restricted area."

"You were there, inside."

"True, but I did not pass a restricted sign."

"I told you. You were seen driving into the area."

"Colonel, you have a wise Russian proverb: The truth is brighter than the sun. It must be a German reporting this false information."

"If you didn't drive by a restricted area sign on the road, how could you get there? Fly?"

"I don't know if I should tell you. Can't you accept the truth, so well demonstrated by your proverb?"

"You may admire this Russian proverb, but we have another: Even on the sun there are spots."

"There are no spots on my truth. Have you ever heard the song, 'A Slow Boat to China?' "

"No."

"It's a great song. I took a slow boat."

Saigada gave me a puzzled look and changed the subject to the weather. He returned my identification card and dismissed me. The arrest lasted no more than ten minutes.

That day, 17 August 1960, was a sad one for Gary Powers, but a good one for USMLM intelligence collection and for us. We obtained detailed photographs of a new antenna arrangement, photographed a Soviet Army training area, and took some excellent telephoto pictures of a major East German shipyard and Soviet naval ships under repair. The colonel had understood my reference to a slow boat: a new restriction sign was installed at the entrance to the ferry.

6

The Language Barrier

In the early months of my tour of duty at the USMLM I was shocked by the lack of Russian language proficiency in the mission. No driver spoke Russian. The naval officer whom I relieved, Lt. Cdr. Fred Yates, spoke fluent German but no Russian. Most of the mission's army officers had attended the U.S. Army Language School and a special language program in West Germany, but their lack of proficiency made them unsuitable as interpreters at high-level Russian and American meetings. There were two exceptions, however: U.S. Army lieutenant colonel Charles Fitzgerald (who had attended both the U.S. Army and U.S. Navy Language Schools and had completed a tour of duty as an assistant attaché in Moscow), and U.S. Air Force major Matthew Warren (who had Slavic origins and was also fluent in the language). A thorough knowledge of and fluency in Russian certainly should have been a minimum requirement for the American military leader assigned to conduct liaison with the Soviet Army, but the USMLM chief knew no Russian and no German.

Intelligence collection at the mission was intense, so no one seemed to care that the sign on the pillar at the entrance to the Potsdam House grounds had a spelling error—the Russian word for "headquarters" was spelled incorrectly. Since the Russian alphabet represents sounds phonetically, there never will be a Russian spelling bee. Yet, the glaring error on that sign could have been corrected by changing one letter. When I approached the USMLM chief about correcting the sign his reaction was, "Fella, if it's already on the pillar, it must be right!" How long the error existed for all to see during the forty-three years that the USMLM existed, I do not know. The word was spelled incorrectly when I arrived and it was spelled incorrectly when I left.

Other USMLM army officers had major problems with the Russian language due to a lack of depth in their knowledge of Russian idioms, expressions, proverbs, and folklore. One can have mental access to an extensive Russian vocabulary and yet still not have a clue about what is being said in Russian. My first knowledge of this shortcoming occurred when I observed a conversation between Soviet lieutenant colonel Khortov and several mission officers.

Khortov said, "We are going to show you where the crawfish winter." The army officers had no idea whether this was good or bad. (It means "we are going to make trouble for you.")

Before long other examples appeared and it became obvious that none of the mission personnel had the slightest idea of the meaning when a Russian said, "You have exchanged a cuckoo for a hawk" ("You have miscalculated"); or "Your conduct is a bear's service" ("Your clumsy but well-intended action is only causing more problems"); or "You are taking your words from the ceiling" ("You're talking through your hat"). Some other often-repeated but equally misunderstood phrases include: "Let's not cook the kasha, let's eat it" ("Let's not stir up trouble. Let's clear up the mess"); "The matter is written on the water with a pitchfork" ("The matter is still up in the air"); and "I'm not trying to tease the geese" ("I'm not trying to annoy you"). These expressions, which caused many problems for USMLM officers, illustrate the fact that it is not enough to simply understand the words of a foreign language.

I was fortunate to have had fourteen years of close association with the Russian language before I reported to the USMLM. After graduating from high school in 1941 I entered the U.S. Navy's flight training program. During World War II I flew airships on antisubmarine patrols. In early 1946 my naval reserve commission was terminated and on 15 June of that year I accepted a commission in the regular navy. To allow me to earn the equivalent education of a Naval Academy graduate, the U.S. Navy sent me to Brown University in Rhode Island. The navy advised me to take the math, science, and foreign language courses of my choosing. In the fall of 1946 Brown University for the first time offered a course on the Russian language. I came to believe that Russian would be the most essential foreign language for a naval officer to be fluent in during the coming postwar years, and enrolled in Russian 101. After two-and-a-half years of learning Russian at Brown I was accepted into the navy's intensive immersion Russian program in Washington, D.C. After an additional year of learning from a dozen native Russian professors I was qualified as an interpreter and translator of the Russian language. When the navy decided to fly airships from aboard aircraft carriers on hunter-killer operations, any assignments making use of my Russian were thwarted by orders I received to return to lighter-than-air duty. Even after I had completed the navy's postgraduate intelligence course in 1953, I did not receive the same orders to intelligence duty as others had. After completing the course I was sent to Pensacola, Florida, for heavier-than-air flight training. Regardless of the lack of opportunities to use the Russian language while assigned to various duty stations, I continued to improve my Russian language knowledge through self-directed focus and study.

Finally in 1957 I received orders assigning me to the staff of the U.S. Naval Intelligence School in Washington, D.C. After recognizing my proficiency in Russian, the school's director selected me to head the language division, where nine foreign languages were taught to naval officers assigned to attaché posts and to other navy personnel with special linguistic needs.

The Russian department was the largest in the school, though at the time there was a dearth of proficient Russian linguists in Washington. Once again I had the opportunity to speak Russian on a daily basis. Besides my teaching duties, other opportunities to interpret abounded, including interrogation sessions with Soviet captain Nicholas Fedorovich Artamonov, the highest-ranking active Soviet naval officer to defect to the United States. After three years of daily involvement with the Russian language at the school, I departed for the USMLM. The officers there, I was disappointed to learn, had only a rudimentary ability with the Russian language. The deplorable situation gave me the opportunity to participate as an interpreter during high-level exchanges between the U.S. and Soviet commanders in chief. At those meetings Marsh. Ivan Konev insisted that everyone seated at the negotiation table be a delegate with authority to speak on his own. As a result five of us—Gen. Bruce Clark, his deputy, the USMLM chief, the USMLM deputy Lieutenant Colonel Fitzgerald, and I—sat across from Marshal Konev and his four cronies. On our side Fitzgerald and I did most of the talking. On the Soviet side Marshal Konev monopolized the dialogue. The other Americans at the table never understood what Fitzgerald and I were saying in Russian (though we did accurately interpret Konev's remarks to General Clark). Final decisions were always made by Konev and Clark.

There was no question that USMLM army officers were highly effective in field operations. Language proficiency was not as critical to reconnaissance as it was to liaison operations. The courage and bravery of U.S. Amy mission officers and men operating as close as one can get to combat conditions without waging total war were exemplary. I often thanked God that Sgt. Mel Ratz and other mission personnel were on our side.

One incident in the field illustrates the value of having had both personal initiative and Russian language proficiency when it came to coping with difficult situations in East Germany. East German air space was violated by a U.S. Air Force C-47 plane on 20 May 1960. That same month the Soviets had downed an American U-2 plane conducting a fly-over of the Soviet Union and a private French sports plane had invaded East German air space. The French violation on 5 May drew a strong written protest from Gen. Ivan Yakubovsky, commander in chief of the Group of Soviet Forces–Germany: "I want to draw your attention to the fact that Soviet troops in East Germany, in accordance with the Warsaw Treaty, could have taken measures against the aircraft preventing it from flying over East Germany with immunity. . . . The Soviet Command in the future will be forced to [take] the . . . strongest measures for curbing any future violations of the airspace of East Germany."

Only fifteen days later, while en route from Denmark to its home base in Libya, another American air force C-47 plane violated East German airspace and was forced down by Soviet fighters in the northern part of the country. Five crew members and four passengers were detained. Gen. Clyde D. Eddleman, commander of the U.S. Army–Europe, contacted Yakubovsky requesting the "immediate return" of the Americans. The USMLM dispatched its deputy chief, Lt. Col. Clark Baldwin, and its air team chief, Maj. Matthew Warren, to the scene to evaluate the situation and to arrange for the release of the passengers by bus to West Berlin.

On-site negotiations with the Soviets resulted in a simple solution: since Warren was a qualified C-47 pilot, the Soviets, with U.S. Air Force approval, permitted Warren to fly the downed aircraft and all the captives out of East Germany. On 25 May, the day of the plane's departure, Baldwin and Warren, along with the original C-47 pilot and two Soviet colonels, signed a protocol. The plane, crew, and passengers were promptly released and flew directly to Wiesbaden, West Germany. In view of Yakubovsky's earlier protest and severe warning it is doubtful that the violation could have been handled so expeditiously had the USMLM not been accredited to Yakubovsky's command. Knowledge of the Soviet psyche and Warren's Russian language proficiency saved the day.

Throughout my tour of duty I felt sorry for mission members who lacked sufficient Russian language ability. It was a barrier that stopped them from participating in extremely interesting and high-level exchanges with the Soviets and forced them to endure less enjoyable and more stressful detentions. However, nothing obstructed their aggressive reconnaissance tasks, always made at great personal risk, which provided superior intelligence to the United States during the cold war.

One must be familiar with Russian fairy tales and proverbs to communicate on a level of understanding that leads to successful negotiations and meaningful exchanges with Russians. During the height of the cold war, that is, from 1960 to 1962, no place held more importance for ensuring that both sides knew what the other side was saying than the Soviet Zone in East Germany. Because the contemporary Russian language evolved from the early peasant spoken language, the meaning of expressions in Russian can be especially cryptic for English speakers of the world. The simple world of Russian peasants produced a language rich with earthy vocabulary. Fauna also plays a major role in contemporary speech, as well as in Russian fairy tales and proverbs. Most acclaimed of Russian fabulists was I. A. Krylov, whose works were distinguished by their wisdom and humor. The typical moral of a Krylov fable does not preach abstract reason, but rather an inevitable inference from the described episode.

In order to explain the need for cooperation in international affairs, two U.S. presidents—John Kennedy and Ronald Reagan—used to their advantage the Krylov fairy tale about the pike, the swan, and the crab all pulling in different directions and failing to make headway. Ronald Reagan used the fable in his December 1987 summit with Gorbachev. President Kennedy used the same fable earlier to describe Khrushchev's attempt to replace Dag Hammarskjöld (the United Nations secretary general killed in a 1961 plane crash) with three presiding secretaries who would share the office with equal power.

President Kennedy called attention to the fairy tale to point out to Khrushchev the merit of having one secretary general rather than three. A Russian troika is usually pulled by three horses, but Krylov wrote of the plight of another three, pulling at cross-purposes:

> A swan, a pike, and a crab took to their station
> In harness and would drag a loaded cart.
> But when came the moment for them to start,
> They sweat, they strain, and yet the cart
> Stands still; what's lacking?
> The load must, as it seemed, have been but light;
> The swan through to the clouds takes flight,
> The pike to the water pulls, the crab keeps backing.
> Now which of them was right, which wrong, concerns us not;
> The cart is still upon the selfsame spot.

Not long after the president presented his version of the tale to the Russians, Khrushchev abandoned his effort to establish a "troika" in the United Nations.

Folklore can be the ultimate buttress to use in reinforcing one side of a disagreement among Russians. Since it is understood to be the absolute wisdom of the Russian peasant's soul, it can be used in every circumstance from everyday family life predicaments to high-level negotiations. Find a fairy tale or a proverb to prove a point, and the argument is won, hands down. Proverbs are especially valuable because there are so many available. One well versed in Russian proverbs can find a proverb to fit almost any situation.

As a result of collections gathered in the late seventeenth and early eighteenth centuries, thousands of proverbs have been passed to the present generation. The first special publication of proverbs in the Russian press occurred in 1769 or 1770, when M. D. Chukov wrote "A Collection of 4,291 Ancient Russian Proverbs." A significant number of these proverbs had appeared earlier in the Russian press, but not together in a collection. Although many Russian proverbs were printed in the eighteenth and nineteenth centuries, they nevertheless all belong to the earlier verbal customs of the peasant people and not the written traditions of later times.

A few proverbs are understood the same in both the English and Russian languages, such as "There's not smoke without fire." Others express the same idea with different words: President Truman said that "if you can't stand the heat, get out of the kitchen," while a Russian would say, "If you are afraid of wolves, don't go into the forest." The saying "When in Rome, do as the Romans do" is spoken by Russians as "Live with wolves, howl like wolves." "Making a camel out of a flea" is, of course, the same as "making a mountain out of a molehill." Many Russian proverbs have no English equivalent: "A goose and a pig are not comrades"; "Red apples are not grown for a wolf"; "Be friends with a wolf, but carry an axe"; "There is no honor in a beard, even a goat has one."

One of the most difficult challenges in high-level liaison exchanges and for me in my personal detentions was to have a second or third proverb ready if a Russian was clever enough to rebut a given argument with a proverb of his own. There was a great feeling of satisfaction when I "had the last proverb." Even during the many times I didn't succeed, altercations ended with a laugh and tensions were eased.

Successful reconnaissance required living unseen by the Russian military in the German forests. The Russians have a proverb to fit this complication: "A nightingale lives in the forest with a crow, but both sing different songs." When caught in the forest I found it most advantageous to, as closely as possible, sing the same song.

7

Fall 1960 Liaison and Collection

Before my arrival at USMLM the chief of the mission was replaced under mysterious emergency circumstances that involved an alleged family transgression. The deputy chief, Lt. Col. Clark Baldwin, U.S. Army, served as acting chief until a replacement arrived. Under Baldwin my collection effort flourished as I uncovered a number of new Soviet military dispositions and sighted a mobile military decontamination unit, something never before seen in the Soviet forces.

The comradeship that I found among my army colleagues diminished quickly in the summer of 1960 upon the arrival of the new chief. On the new chief's first day the mission's civilian secretary telephoned my office, upset by what she had heard the colonel say to the new deputy chief, Lt. Col. Charles Fitzgerald: "Find a way to get rid of that navy S.O.B.!" Fitz, as he was called, tried to convince the colonel that I worked as hard as any member, wore army field and OG uniforms on reconnaissance tours, and had already established my reputation as a superb photographer. The colonel persisted: "We don't need a sailor here. Work his butt off until he slips up. Get me a reason to kick his ass out of here."

The day after this conversation took place I encountered the colonel at our backup headquarters in West Berlin. The chief hollered, "Put a patch on that navy uniform, fella. Nobody in my unit is properly dressed without a USMLM patch on his shoulder."

"I can't do that, Colonel. A patch isn't permitted by the navy's uniform regulations."

"Don't give me any back talk, fella, do it! In the fall you will be in the company of the commander in chief, U.S. Army–Europe. Everyone under my command will wear the USMLM patch, no exceptions."

The last thing I wanted was a patch sewn onto my navy uniform. On occasions when I visited cities and East German industrial fairs I wore my navy uniform. After two years at Brown University, one year as a student among native speakers at the navy's Foreign Language School, and three years as director of the school, my Russian proficiency was flawless. I found that Soviet Air Force and Army officers had no idea that I was a foreign officer. I was always amazed by their lack of recognition of the uniform of their sister service, the Soviet Navy. They mistook me for one of their own and talked freely about their units, their morale, and other useful information. I struck up conversations at every opportunity. I knew that wearing the USMLM patch, which contained an American flag, would bring these most enjoyable strokes of good fortune and interesting intelligence collection abruptly to an end.

I finally came up with an idea: write a letter to the navy's chief of the Bureau of Naval Personnel in Washington, via the chain of command which included the chief, U.S. Military Liaison Mission to the Group of Soviet Forces–Germany, and the commander in chief, U.S. Naval Forces–Europe. The USMLM chief could put his comments on the request before forwarding the letter to the commander in chief for his endorsement. I was convinced that Adm. Harold Page Smith at headquarters in London would write his disapproval in strong language before forwarding the letter to Washington, since there certainly were no senior naval officers who would recommend a change in navy uniform regulations. I handed my letter to the colonel for his endorsement.

The colonel was in a bind. He wanted me to attend the official visit between the commander in chief, U.S. Army–Europe and the commander in chief, Soviet Forces–Germany, and use my Russian language proficiency, but he would not budge about wanting to see a patch on the naval uniform. After reading my letter the chief said, "If this isn't approved, fella, you're out of here!"

"It's the best I can do, Colonel."

In a week I received a copy of Admiral Smith's endorsement in his forwarding letter to Rear Admiral W. R. Smedberg III, chief of naval personnel in Washington, which stated: "Disapproved. The U.S. naval uniform is sufficiently distinctive without a patch." No way was I going to show this to the colonel before the final reply was received from the chief of naval personnel. After three weeks of apprehension I could hardly wait to get into the envelope addressed to me from Washington. The message was brief: "Commander Fahey is authorized to wear a patch at his own discretion. He may wear it when and where he decides it is appropriate to do so."

I did not expect this response from Rear Admiral Smedberg, a two-star admiral, because by giving me permission to wear the USMLM patch he had overruled the decision of a four-star admiral, Harold Page Smith. I was grateful for Admiral Smedberg's wording because it gave me the flexibility to wear the patch as I saw fit.

The USMLM chief also received a copy of the reply and called me to his office. "Sew the patch on, fella. Now, today!"

The U.S. Military Liaison Mission patch was sewn on the dress blue navy uniform that I wore when I traveled in West Berlin. While in East Germany on liaison assignments I also wore the uniform with the patch. When I traveled around the country to collect intelligence information in Soviet Zone cities, however, I wore my other set of dress blues with no patch. I was able to pass myself off as a Russian or other Warsaw Pact naval officer in the Soviet Zone. Intelligence reports on Soviet Army and Soviet Air Force units that I created from my conversations with Soviet personnel in East German cities continued. During reconnaissance trips in the field (which were mostly in the woods and off the beaten tracks), I wore army clothing.

The colonel never knew the difference. I wore the uniform with the patch when I accompanied him on all liaison assignments. He thought that I always wore the patch when dressed in my naval uniform and once commented, "It took a while, but we got that straightened out, fella. It looks good and it saved your ass!"

Despite my first frosty skirmish with the new USMLM chief, he recognized my language abilities and assigned me to work with Lieutenant Colonel Fitzgerald as an interpreter at all liaison and emergency meetings with the Russians. The chief neither spoke nor understood Russian or German so when he had one-on-one talks with the Russians, Fitzgerald would be the sole interpreter. At high-level meetings interpretation was a critical need. Our generals did not know Russian and the Soviet marshal and generals spoke no English.

The first high-level meeting that I attended between the commander in chief, U.S. Army–Europe and the commander in chief, Soviet Forces–Germany, was both useful and fascinating. Both army commanders were accompanied by staff members. The meeting was held at the Soviet headquarters in Zossen-Wunsdorf, the same complex occupied by the German general staff during World War II. The meeting began with a tour by a convoy of limousines to the Battle Field of Nations, the site where the Russians and their allies defeated Napoleon. The most amusing sight on the trip was when the dozen or more expensive vehicles stopped by the side of the road to allow their military occupants to relieve their bladders.

The two-day affair gave the opportunity for the commanders and their staffs to establish a good relationship. When freed from our interpreting duties, some Soviet junior officers escorted Fitzgerald and me around selected areas of the headquarters. We toured the palatial residence of the Soviet commander in chief, which housed all sorts of treasures including a posh billiard room. (I was surprised by the pool table's tiny balls and big pockets.) We then visited a Soviet colonel's home to find another colonel's family living on the second floor. These family members had to reach their residence through the downstairs living room. The vast disparity between the general's quarters and field-grade officers' quarters was unexpected, especially in a society that claimed to be classless.

A visit to the mess hall satisfied one intelligence question I had, to find out how many Soviet soldiers were in a squad. Every table there had eleven chairs, one at the head of the table and five on each side. Fitz said, "We've got it! They are eating by squads." It seemed logical: the squad leader sat at the head of the table. Our questions were greeted by blank stares, so the observation went unconfirmed. I don't know if Fitz's intelligence report sent later was evaluated well, but in 1970 I learned from some personal research of Soviet military papers that a Soviet squad indeed consists of eleven members.

The official visit gave me the opportunity to gather information for a lengthy intelligence report. During a stop on the way to the Battle of Nations site a Soviet military doctor noticed a problem in my right eye (continual weeping had begun without warning from a blocked tear duct). Once we arrived back at the headquarters the doctor insisted that I be taken to the base hospital. Soviet security personnel tried to intervene, but after a prolonged argument the doctor prevailed. On the way to the hospital we passed all sorts of military trappings, including guns and a camouflaged anti-aircraft missile. I regretted that I could reproduce the sightings from my memory only.

At the hospital I was ushered into a large room and left alone. I peeked under the covers that concealed some odd medical equipment. Finally an extremely heavy woman wearing a blood-stained white apron appeared. Although I tried to emphasize that the problem was only in my right eye, she examined both eyes and insisted on applying strong drops of liquid in the left as well as the right eye. To all my protests she responded, "For balance! For balance!" I was prepared to contribute one eye to the cause, but was very unhappy about offering two. She gave me a bottle of the eyedrops, which I did not use again. Upon my return to Berlin I sent the liquid along with my report of the visit to the appropriate U.S. Army authorities. When we rejoined the others my excursion was greeted by the Americans as a coup, believing I had faked my problem to scoop them in a collection effort. Actually it was a fortuitous tear duct blockage.

The evening banquet turned out to be the bash of all bashes. Gen. Ivan Yakubovsky and Gen. Bruce Clark, among other general officers, sat in the center of a long head table raised on a dais. Below at an equally long table sat field-grade officers, all facing the head table. I was located at the extreme right end of the lower table next to a Soviet colonel. Attractive young girls served vodka.

When all were seated the toasts began. Most were initiated by General Yakubovsky and returned, when appropriate, by General Clark. Yakubovsky and Clark sipped their drinks. Everyone but me followed Yakubovsky's orders to drink bottoms up (in Russian: "To the bottom!") at every toast. Fish was served and the toasts continued.

Yakubovsky would smile and shout, "To the bottom! Keep those fish swimming!" The Soviet officer on my left dutifully finished his vodka at every urging. The female waiters filled every glass between each toast. With a broad, friendly smile the pretty girl serving me put just a drop in my glass every time.

Because I was at the end of the table no one but the Soviet colonel on my left could see that I was not drinking on each occasion. At first the colonel was conversant. By about the tenth toast he began to ask me if Vice President Nixon, whom he greatly admired, really believed in God. When I said that yes, Nixon did believe in God, the Soviet began to slobber a story about his mother taking him to church when he was a child. He wanted me to confirm for him that God existed.

Abruptly, when Yakubovsky offered a toast to the citizens of both countries, the colonel staggered to his feet and in a booming, slurred voice complained to Yakubovsky and Clark that I had not drank to the bottom as he had during all the toasts. As they say, the silence was deafening. General Clark frowned. (Scowled might be a better word.) Yakubovsky asked, "It this true? You haven't kept the fish swimming? They are lying dead in your dry belly?"

I rose and in Russian replied, "Gospodin General, it seems to me that we have had toasts to the glorious Soviet and American armies, tank divisions, artillery, engineers, air forces, World War II snipers, and even civilians, but not one toast to the navy. I will drink to the bottom a toast to the navy, and to all other toasts. I challenge my Russian friend beside me to bottoms up every drink with me."

Having not understood a word I had said, General Clark continued to glare at me. The colonel next to me protested and sniveled bitterly that this was not the question, but Yakubovsky shouted, "To the navies of the world!" Both the colonel and I were now standing as all the seated Russians chanted in unison, "To the bottom! To the bottom! To the bottom!" General Clark's scowl disappeared. Yakubovsky appeared happy to have more toasts available, and proceeded to toast the U.S. Navy and then the Soviet Navy, followed by, "Dinner is served."

After dinner we adjourned to separate tables of four officers each for dessert and brandy. At my table I found one Russian officer who hadn't had a single drink, a major general who complained that he had ulcers. Not feeling any pain myself, I forced him to bottoms up a brandy with me.

The next day a special trip had to be made back to the Soviet headquarters by air force captain Jack Pendergast to retrieve a certain American colonel's false teeth. After having placed them beside his bed before he slept, he awoke in the morning and then drove to Berlin without them—further evidence that everyone had had a great time at the banquet.

In September 1960 the frequency of USMLM reconnaissance tours accelerated. The Soviet army operated on a training schedule that began a new cycle of classroom training on 1 December every year. The intensity and scope of training increased during the year, as early basic training was followed by platoon drills and regimental skirmishes. Eventually the Soviet forces in East Germany divided into two armies, east and west, which waged all-out war before the end of the annual training cycle in November.

In the fall the Soviet troop movements became our number one priority. It was not unusual to return after thirty-six hours to my residence in West Berlin, ashen white from lack of sleep, only to be awakened and called to return to the Soviet Zone a few hours later. Yet there was much intelligence to be gathered when the Soviet forces were active. Once, in the early weeks of my USMLM reconnaissance tours, I had seen new equipment but then had drawn such a poor sketch that no one would accept my sighting. Quickly I learned to photograph every possible target, taking hundreds of pictures on every trip.

In the early fall I found a Soviet disposition of howitzers and guns that the U.S. military had never seen before. By working my way to several excellent but concealed observation points at the edge of the woods I was able to photograph the entire grouping. In 1960 there were no spy satellites and the spy on the ground had no competitor.

In October of that year, while walking along the banks of the Elbe River, I had observed and photographed a group of Soviet T-54 medium tanks crossing the river underwater using snorkels.

The snorkel, a vertical tube that permitted engine air intake and exhaust, also provided ventilation and permitted the tank to submerge and cross along the river bed at snorkel depth. Always less sophisticated, Russians simply called these snorkels "pipes." The tank's capability surprised me. All that could be seen were six pipes moving slowly through the water from the bank on my side to the opposite bank. A winch, visible on the other side, apparently was used for unexpected emergencies.

Ten years later, in the early seventies, I came across a Soviet book about Soviet underwater tanks that provided some aspects of the vehicle's operation not known to me when I had made my earlier visual observation. The tanks often were not watertight and ventilation was difficult because of the many other demands placed on the snorkel (especially engine intake and exhaust). In that situation it was a challenge to keep the crew's morale high, and on occasion some crew members would suffer panic attacks or claustrophobia.

In November 1960 the Soviets issued temporary restriction maps to the American, the British, and the French liaison missions. Entry into a previously open and expansive territory was henceforth strictly forbidden. Generally the maps were ignored and did not keep us from following Soviet military movements.

As the training war between the two Soviet armies progressed, I had little trouble finding the front line because it always moved from east to west. There was never a possibility that the west army would win. If I temporarily lost track of a battle, I could always find the action by sighting a simulated mushroom cloud. Or, whenever a Soviet squad or other unit landed on a riverbank, the men would shout, "oo-RAH! oo-RAH! oo-RAH!" Their shouts would thunder through the woods and help me locate the action just as I was ready to give up the chase. I never doubted that the Soviets would use tactical nuclear weapons in an actual conflict because I saw with my own eyes that tactical nuclear weapons were part of their training.

Every day in the fall was like every other: follow the Soviet troops and report. I was never detained during these surveillance trips. Later in the fall and winter of 1960 I encountered two distractions in West Berlin, one of which was serious enough to eventually change the USMLM chief's status as my commanding officer. The other arose from my personal support of John F. Kennedy in the election for president of the United States.

8

KENNEDY FOR PRESIDENT

Almost as one, army officers at both the USMLM and at the Berlin command were strong supporters of Vice President Richard Nixon for president. Anointed by President Eisenhower and beloved by the army officers, Nixon was the overwhelming choice.

Before leaving for Germany in May 1960 I had made arrangements for students attending a new program established at the U.S. Navy Language School to visit some Washington dignitaries. In addition to the nine foreign languages taught at the school, English classes were given to foreign military and civilian personnel from friendly countries of the free world. Since few of these students had ever previously visited the United States and were unfamiliar with our customs and government, I enlisted the services of Washington VIPs who I thought could best communicate our country's various branches of government. Sen. John Kennedy agreed to talk to our incoming students about the legislative branch.

Kennedy was most generous with his time, but we wondered whether he and I were having a private dialogue because with their limited knowledge of English the foreign officers had little to say. Despite many campaign demands, however, Senator Kennedy spent about forty minutes telling our foreign students about the U.S. government and the history of our country. I was impressed with his good nature, quick wit, and the special hospitality that he gave to us during our visit to his office. He was running for president of the United States and I planned to vote for him.

Being attached to the USMLM in the fall 1960, during the height of the presidential campaign, meant that I was cut off from all television news, including the two Kennedy-Nixon debates that had already been held. When Kennedy campaigners scheduled a rally at the Berlin Hilton in West Berlin, I relished the chance to attend. The organizers set up drinks and food, showed the first two debates on video, and offered Kennedy campaign bumper stickers, hats, and buttons. The Berlin rally was not a great success. I was surprised to find that in addition to campaign personnel only four people were present: a German, a Catholic priest, my wife Barbara, and me. Despite the meager turnout, we Kennedy backers were upbeat and extremely optimistic.

The Soviet military was flippant and sometimes outright nasty about the American election. In 1960 Soviet officers showed no respect for either presidential candidate, but later their attitudes changed. When Kennedy was assassinated the Soviet people of Leningrad were saddened to the point of playing funeral music on a loudspeaker all day without permission. Nevertheless, during his presidency Nixon was an overwhelming favorite among Soviet leaders. During one of my later visits to the Soviet Union officials in Volgograd invited my study group to a plush Party headquarters location to lament the possibilities of Nixon's impeachment.

One episode during the presidential pre-election days had the potential to cause an international incident. In late fall of 1960 the British liaison mission hosted a reception in the British sector of Berlin. French, American, and Soviet officers were invited. On similar occasions Russians had always stayed in a group and were rarely left alone—a security person was always on hand to carefully watch all the others. At the reception air force captain Jack Pendergast and I were discussing the close surveillance of each Russian officer by another Soviet officer when I boasted that I could place a Kennedy button on the uniform of Soviet colonel Kozlovsky without being noticed or caught in the act. Jack dared me to try.

I quietly moved next to Kozlovsky and carefully pinned a Kennedy button near the left shoulder of his uniform. I was close enough to Kozlovsky's side to block anyone from seeing me do it, then I slowly moved away before Kozlovsky saw me.

Within a couple of minutes Lieutenant Zhelanov approached Kozlovsky and removed the Kennedy button. All the Russians immediately herded together and marched out of the building into the street. As they weren't privy to the reason for the abrupt departure, the British hosts voiced their anger at the Russians' sudden withdrawal. I found Jack, the only other person who knew why the Russians had bolted from the room. As we talked about my obligation to tell the British, a half dozen Russians returned and resumed their conversations as though nothing had happened.

One Brit commented, "How odd. Glad to see the chaps back again."

Ten minutes passed before Kozlovsky approached me. "I've got a present for you."

"Fine, Colonel, let me have it."

Kozlovsky pushed the pin into the palm of my right hand, drawing a little blood. "Thanks, Colonel, but keep it as a gift, or give it to your children."

"No thanks, Commander, it will be worthless in a few days."

The party continued happily. The British considered the affair a huge success. I learned that Zhelanov was certainly a GRU (army intelligence) officer who kept close tabs on his colleagues. I also learned to keep Kennedy buttons in my pocket.

Although I was sure that no one saw me pin Kozlovsky, during their deliberations on the street the Russians had concluded that I was the culprit. I found Jack Pendergast to be a good friend who could keep a secret. No one found out about my rather foolish prank.

On election day I was on a mission deep inside East Germany and did not know until much later that John Kennedy had won the election.

9

On the Lighter Side

After a day of reconnaissance inside East Germany on election eve 1960, I decided to overnight in the north. We entered a crowded and noisy Rostock restaurant on the Baltic coast for dinner.

My colleague on the trip was a mission officer, Major M., who led the good life and never missed an opportunity for pleasure. On trips to East Germany he overnighted in the largest cities, ate, drank, and slept in the best hotels, and always enjoyed to the fullest the fruits of the relatively barren people's republic. To his credit he was one of the most aggressive and effective collectors of intelligence working in the USMLM. Possession of this greatly admired talent didn't interfere with his delightful evening sojourns.

No one paid attention to us as we threaded our way to a table near the band, a sight to behold. The seven-piece orchestra of middle-aged and elderly men were dressed in tuxedos. They played music that was soft and pleasant. One would never have guessed that we were dining in a communist country.

Before partaking of a delicious rump steak dinner, Major M. approached the little stage and whispered a few words to the orchestra leader, who kept a divided eye on his charges as he bent over to hear my colleague. The elderly gentleman nodded assent, and M. returned to our table. Soon a waiter arrived with a menu and two miniature American flags for a centerpiece. "They know me here," said Major M., pushing himself back proudly.

"American flags on the table," I gasped. "We don't even legally recognize their country."

"You ain't seen nothin' yet, as the man says," replied the major.

A short time later I was astounded to hear the initial strains of the "Star Spangled Banner." I leaped to rigid attention. The babble of voices didn't slacken as no one else paid heed to the music or to my action.

"How can they get away with that?" I asked. "There are police, German soldiers, and a few Russian officers in here."

"John, you still don't understand the Communist society. You're out in the woods all of the time. The action is in the cities."

"I know. I know. But how can they play our national anthem, unless they don't know what it is? Most of our people wouldn't recognize theirs."

"The band knows what it plays and so do half the people in here. It doesn't matter."

"If an American band suddenly played the Soviet national anthem and Americans knew what it was, there would be bedlam."

"You don't understand the people's state. This is not the United States. Over the entire Soviet Zone of Germany the law is the same: 60 percent Communist-originated music to a maximum of 40 percent music from the West. Within the 40 percent allowed they can play anything. No restrictions."

I was giving this some thought when Major M. asked, "Any requests?"

"Do they know 'Yankee Doodle Dandy?' "

"They love it!"

Secretary Joan called. "The colonel wants you on the double!"

Upon entering the colonel's office I couldn't believe my eyes. Cases of bourbon were stacked from floor to ceiling. "I'm going to have four senior USMLM officers visit Soviet kommandants and deliver Christmas presents from me. You are going to cover the north."

"Colonel, these Soviet officers don't celebrate Christmas and most of their offices are in the cities where East Germans will see us. They like us and hate the Russians. It's great for German morale when Germans see us dragged into these Soviet kommandants' headquarters, accused of espionage, but seeing us bringing presents to the Russians will be a real downer."

"No discussion. Take two cases, fella, and get a driver. Don't come back with one bottle!"

I told the driver to proceed to Perleberg, the location of a Soviet junior kommandant who served under a more senior kommandant in Ludwigslust. The Perleberg kommandant met us with open arms. "Welcome. You've come to learn about our glorious socialist system. Both of our countries are working for peace and friendship. I am delighted that you stopped by."

Handing him a bottle of bourbon, I said, "No, Colonel. I dropped by to give you some booze for Christmas from our mission chief."

Grabbing the bottle tightly, the kommandant replied, "You are most kind, but we don't observe Christmas."

"Well, then, for the greatest of your holidays, New Year's."

"Some of our people believe New Year's Day to be the greatest holiday. However, the most glorious celebration for me is October Revolution Day, on November seventh."

"Fine, consider it a belated Revolution Day gift. Happy holiday!"

I left as soon as I could without offending his hospitality. Before I departed he asked me to return at another time for a discussion about the progress of the capitalist world as it moved toward socialism.

The kommandant's headquarters were located close to a firing range, so I decided to check out the range. As I had expected, the range was vacant because a new Soviet training cycle had begun on 1 December. I observed a platoon without weapons marching toward the range. Most of the soldiers were new recruits with shaved heads. Learning to march was the first priority of the new training year.

About an hour passed before I was back on Route 5 proceeding north to Ludwigslust. Thirty minutes after that we saw our dedicated Perleberg kommandant barreling south on Route 5 in a GAZ-69 (a vehicle similar to our Jeep). We learned the reason for his rush when we arrived in Ludwigslust.

The Ludwigslust kommandant, a full colonel, escorted me into his office and invited me to have a drink of bourbon from a half empty bottle. The Perleberg officer had rushed to Ludwigslust to present the gift we had given him to his senior officer, who wasted no time in guzzling half the bottle.

"I appreciate your holiday present. As a colonel, do I get two bottles?"

"Sure. Excuse me, Colonel, I left a second bottle in the car." I returned to the office with another fifth, politely refused to join the colonel in his morning drinking bout, then continued north to Hagenow.

At the Hagenow kommandantura the on-duty officer demanded my mission pass and led me into a detention room. After half an hour a Soviet colonel entered the room and asked what was the purpose of my visit.

"A present from my chief for the forthcoming winter holidays."

"Who's your chief, and who are you?"

"Colonel, your duty officer has my identification. I'm an American member of your army."

"You're a spy, like the others we have caught here around our military installations."

"Colonel, I really am here on a goodwill mission."

"Get out of here! We want nothing from you."

"I can't leave without my pass."

"Get his pass and get him out of here!"

"Colonel, you can be sure that I'll tell General Yakubovsky about your warm hospitality."

"You know General Yakubovsky?"

"We've had a few drinks together on occasion."

"Our general is a hero of the Soviet Union."

I countered, "And a hero of socialist labor, a member of the Supreme Soviet, a member of the Central Committee of the Communist Party, a commander in the defense of Moscow, and a hero of the battles of Stalingrad and Kursk."

"You know about him."

Referring to Yakubovsky by his first name and patronymic, normally used only by close friends, I added, "I know him. Ivan Ignatevich stormed Berlin and liberated Prague. As my commander in chief he is an inspiration to me."

"You like him?"

"I do have one complaint about him."

"What complaint!"

"When we eat and drink vodka together he entices me to drink too much by saying, 'Don't stop! Drink to the bottom! You must keep those fish swimming down there.'"

"You do know Ivan Ignatevich. I'll take your gift. But next time bring vodka. You can come back. But tell your other American friends to stop hanging around here. Goodbye!"

My driver had begun to think that I would never return. I explained that these visits were getting to be fun.

Next stop: Rostock. The Soviet duty officer, a captain, greeted me at the door and informed me that the kommandant was not available.

"I have a present for him."

"He's not here."

"Please take it and give it to him."

"Sorry, I cannot."

"I saw a light in his office."

"He's out."

"I can wait."

"He won't be back for days."

"I can wait."

"He's in the hospital."

"I can go anywhere. Where's the hospital? I'll visit him."

"He cannot have visitors."

"Will you hold this bottle for a minute, please?"

As soon as the captain took the bottle I said good-bye and left.

After arriving back in Potsdam I learned that the chief also had visited some Soviet kommandants and had managed to deliver two bottles. The fact that I brought back six bottles didn't seem to trouble him. Later I told him to be sure to include me in the next year's run to deliver Christmas cheer. He replied, "We won't be giving presents next year." I never did find out whether his visits succeeded, but since the colonel didn't know a word of Russian, I imagine they weren't great triumphs.

10

The Stasi Shooting

The night before a U.S. Air Force team arrived for a four-day inspection tour of mission facilities in West Berlin, the chief and his operations officer advised me that I was to conduct a five-day reconnaissance trip in the Soviet Zone in the company of army captain J. Using the word "reconnaissance" was a questionable way to describe our planned activities in the zone since we were ordered to stay within a limited geographical boundary and to not return until the following Sunday. By suspect coincidence our scheduled return followed the departure of the team of inspectors. The colonel had experienced difficulties with Major Warren and his air force team before and no doubt he did not want me questioned during the inspectors' visit.

J., a wiry, high-strung officer, was very aggressive and well known for his high speed chases, especially for his ability to keep up with military trains that were transporting missiles. A West Point graduate, J. looked forward to a future brilliant career. Except for an isolated exchange on the possibility of running into some mobile Soviet missiles, J. was a silent traveling companion. He usually traveled with a driver only and, I am sure, was not happy with my company. Neither of us relished the prospect of avoiding contact with the Russians or the German military or the police for five days in the woods. In a country smaller than the state of Tennessee but occupied by hundreds of thousands of Soviet soldiers, avoiding police and security forces was difficult even with maneuvering room. Before our departure I voiced my reservations about carrying out his instructions, but the colonel was adamant in his orders for us to remain in the vicinity of Guestrow, a town approximately 125 miles northwest of Berlin.

We left Berlin at 5:00 P.M., but because we had to drive almost to the coast in a northeasterly direction to skirt a temporarily restricted area, we did not arrive in the Guestrow area until just before dawn. We positioned ourselves in a small patch of woods south of Guestrow between a main road and railroad tracks in order to sight any military traffic passing by. Life in our staff car for three uneventful February days and nights was bitterly cold and boring. When the cold penetrated to the point of numbness we would turn on the engine and heater but, fearing detection, we rarely enjoyed this short-term luxury of warmth. Early in the morning of the fourth day we heard the sporadic roar of motorcycles in a continuing sweep heading generally toward us.

I decided to abandon the patch of woods near the railroad tracks and head for Schwerin, a city of ninety-two thousand about thirty-three miles to the southwest. At daybreak we checked into the Niederlandisch Hotel in Schwerin, showered, and slept soundly until 4:40 P.M. Before dressing I looked out the window and was disappointed to spot an East German surveillance team in a Mercedes 300 parked under a nearby streetlight. Apparently the team had driven all the way from Berlin. A fairly deep snow had enveloped the street.

We reasoned that unless we encountered something special—missiles, perhaps—we would drive directly to mission headquarters in Potsdam. J. wanted to lose the tails, but it seemed pointless to go through the difficulties of losing them unless something important materialized. I mused that if things got exciting that night, at least we had the advantage of having had eight hours of the best sleep that I could ever remember, while the tail had been suffering a long drive on icy roads from East Berlin.

At 6:30 P.M. we left the city with our "friends" tailing us on our rear bumper. The roads were slick but once we were out on the open road J. boosted our speed to fifty miles per hour. We were skidding and sliding, but gradually leaving them farther and farther behind. The tails always tried to stay within one hundred feet of us. We knew that if we could speed ahead to out of their sight, losing them would be a cinch. The infinite possibilities of turns at crossroads would assure us of a tail-less return.

Unfortunately, as we passed through the town of Witzin they closed the gap, and though J. gunned the engine when we reached the east side of town, they pulled up to our left side with ease. Then the vehicle's occupants began to continuously sound the horn and blink the lights. We continued to drive parallel until, skidding and sliding on the icy road, our cars were forced to turn toward the center of the road to avoid slipping into the huge oak trees along both sides of it. The Germans signaled for us to stop by holding out of the car window a "no entry" sign (white circle with a red border). I directed J. to stop.

One of the civilian occupants of the Mercedes approached our car and let loose a tirade of German. He returned to his car and again we both proceeded eastward. After another three miles of honking, blinking lights, and parallel driving, we again collided. Swerving to the right edge of the road close to the bordering trees, J. swung our vehicle to the center and struck the Mercedes, jolting its occupants from side to side. When we broke contact the Mercedes inched forward. Turning the Mercedes wheel to the right and again severely colliding, the Germans were able to bring us to a halt.

Both Germans dashed from the Mercedes and began to abuse us verbally. My demands for identification were ignored.

One Stasi agent returned to his vehicle and began to back up their car flush to our front bumper. The other stood in front of our left headlight.

Suddenly and without warning J. turned the steering wheel left toward the German and stomped down on the accelerator. As the car surged forward the Stasi agent flung himself back and toppled to the ice. As he fell I saw him reach for a pistol under his belt. We had barely cleared the rear of the Mercedes when shots resounded. Our vehicle slid to a stop. The shaken agent on the road scrambled to our car, screaming unintelligibly through the window. The other German leapt from his vehicle and immediately drew a pistol from his trousers. After being certain that we were in the range of one of their weapons, the driver moved the Mercedes against our front bumper.

At 7:10 P.M. a uniformed member of the Volkspolizei arrived on the scene. I heard him inform the agents that our car was a mission vehicle and could not be held at this location. At 7:30 one of the apparently civilian Germans got in the police car and drove westward toward Schwerin. The other German stood on the road training his pistol on us.

After two hours a car stopped about three hundred yards west of our car, and shortly thereafter the German Stasi who had left approached on foot and joined his colleague. The two of them had a ten-minute discussion and then informed us that we could proceed, but to keep our speed below ninety kilometers per hour on the open road and fifty kilometers per hour in towns. The tails pulled ahead, but I directed J. to turn around and return to Schwerin, where the nearest Soviet kommandant was stationed. The Stasi followed us.

When we arrived at the Russian kommandantura, the Stasi parked their car directly behind ours. This was a surprise since Stasi vehicles typically waited discreetly behind a corner or at least a considerable distance down the street when in the vicinity of Russian authorities. The duty sergeant summoned the

Russian duty officer, Captain Akhimov. After presenting my identification card I began my complaint in Russian: "Proceeding east of Witzin we were forcibly stopped and fired upon by two individuals who are now sitting in their vehicle outside your building. I am officially accusing these Germans of this act and request you as the Russian duty officer of the Schwerin kommandantura to place them under arrest."

"They shot at you?"

"Yes."

"Two men now outside?"

"Yes."

The duty officer failed to reach the Russian kommandant by phone. I gave Captain Akhimov the German license number of the surveillance car. Captain Akhimov then called the German criminal police and a Russian-German interpreter. A Soviet captain of the Military Vehicle Inspection Department entered the building with the Stasi driver, followed by the German police officer and an interpreter. The driver was flush with fury and gestured in anger to me.

Captain Akhimov questioned the Stasi agent through the interpreter. "Did you stop these officers?"

"Yes."

"Why?"

"They were speeding."

"Did you shoot at them?"

"No."

"Let me have your identification."

The Stasi agent refused to hand over his identification card to the Russian, but instead showed it to the German policeman. The duty officer then turned to me. "He says that he didn't shoot."

"I understood him. Captain, you didn't ask him if he had a pistol."

Captain Akhimov addressed the German agent, "Do you have a gun?"

"No."

I interrupted, "Why isn't the other hoodlum in here?"

The German became extremely uncomfortable. It was obvious that he didn't understand a word of my conversation with the Russian duty officer. To him it looked like I was in complete control and dictating the interrogation.

The Soviet captain of military vehicle inspection left the room to summon the other German. I couldn't believe what was happening. Although our USMLM chief had complained to the Russians at every opportunity, they always denied having any knowledge of the East Germans' surveillance of our activities. Now the Schwerin duty officer was interrogating them in our presence.

The German passenger denied that he had fired a pistol and was allowed to return to the car. He brought back a black square plastic flashlight which he claimed must have been mistaken for a gun.

"Captain Akhimov," I said, "they both had guns. One of them fired."

After half an hour of continued conversation and interrogation of the Stasi agents, two Soviet officers entered the building and identified themselves as Majors Nizkopoklonny and Kruglov. They shook hands with everyone present then ushered J. and me into the kommandant's office. Captain Akhimov joined us and factually represented our case to Major Nizkopoklonny.

The major asked me, "What's your specific complaint?"

"Two surveillance personnel forcibly stopped us and one fired his gun."

"Impossible!"

"I personally saw both weapons. One was fired at close range."

"Impossible!"

"When you say impossible, you are saying that you don't believe me. Even you Russians respect the truth with a proverb, 'The bitter truth is better than a sweet lie.'"

"Right on! But by impossible I am indicating surprise rather than disbelief."

"Now that you accept that they did this, what are you going to do?"

"We have absolutely no control over what these people do. They are Germans and civilians."

"You know these Germans. They follow us all the time. You Russians deny it, but now they are here in your jurisdiction and have been identified to you."

"It is not a matter of our concern."

"It *is* your concern. We are accredited to your commander in chief. As a liaison officer in the Soviet Army I have reported a serious incident to you and brought the offenders before you for action."

The major swung away for a minute and reflected. Finally he said, "If the incident had involved Soviets, action would be taken by Soviets. This incident involves Germans and therefore should be resolved by German police."

This new tactic took the initiative away from me. Not recognizing the German Democratic Republic, the United States would not tolerate any of its government representatives (me) conducting any discussions or negotiations of an incident with the East Germans. My only hope to regain control was to take the offensive. "If an offense like this had been committed against a Russian, wouldn't you take measures to ensure that it did not reoccur?"

"Why do you always say Russians? We are Soviets! True, I am a Russian. Kruglov and Akhimov are Russians, but many are not Russians. Some are Ukrainians. Some are Armenians. We have many nationalities, but all of us are Soviets. We prefer this."

"Fine," I replied, "I have no objection to calling you Soviets. But your generals don't seem to mind being called Russians. Most seem real proud of their Russian heritage. I've yet to meet a single general or colonel who is not a Russian, although I am sure that there are some. Next time I see General Yakubovsky I'll relay your concern, Major Nizkopoklonny, about using the word 'Russians.' Further, as a major in the Soviet Army I don't think that you have the authority to take action required by such a serious matter."

Nizkopoklonny thought a moment and asked, "I am not familiar with your army rank, 'captain of the second rank,' on your identification card. This means that you are junior to Captain Akhimov?"

"No. I sometimes wear army uniforms in the Soviet Zone, but I am a member of the United States Navy. 'Captain of the second rank' is your Soviet Navy rank used in my identification because I, too, am a Soviet officer. As such, General Yakubovsky prefers to use the Soviet rank for me rather than the American rank, 'commander.'"

"My God! You are senior to both Kruglov and me. That navy rank is equivalent to our army's podpolkovnik rank."

"Yes, and I can make another clarification that would please General Yakubovsky. You have Russians, Ukrainians, Armenians, and many other nationalities, including Americans, French, and British, in the Soviet Army."

Nizkopoklonny greeted this information with silence.

I added: "Neither of us can resolve this at our level. I shall report this incident to my chief for further action. You have investigated the incident, concurred that it occurred, and can inform your superiors who, I'm sure, will be contacted about this affair. My only request to you is that the interrogation of these hoodlums by Captain Akhimov be accurately reported."

"That will be done."

"Now, one other matter. Before leading us into the kommandant's office you gave a signal to a sergeant to release the Germans. These same individuals will follow us to Potsdam. They may shoot again. I request an escort."

Nizkopoklonny answered, "There will be no escort, captain of the second rank, but I can assure you as a Russian officer of a safe return."

We said our farewells. J. drove to the Niederlandisch Hotel, where I called Potsdam. At 12:35 A.M. we started on our way to Potsdam with the black Mercedes traveling close to our rear bumper. Every few miles along the road both cars were stopped by Soviet soldiers for inspection and identification. The Russians were making sure another shooting incident did not occur.

11

Shooting Incident Report

Before noon the following Monday the USMLM chief was in his office, pacing back and forth as he read my report of the Stasi shooting incident. His first remarks were, "I don't like it. I think that your statement about the collision is weak. You say, 'It was my impression that the surveillance car turned into the mission car.' Change it!"

"I'm not sure that they did."

"It's weak, weak! I don't like it. Say they turned into you."

"I saw no deliberate turn into us during the initial collision."

The colonel's face reddened. "Change it, fella! Change it!"

An hour later one of the army mission officers informed me that he had overheard an earlier conversation between the chief and Captain J. in which the two of them were considering firing five shots into our vehicle to show the Russians concrete evidence of the shooting.

I summoned J. to my office. As soon as he crossed the threshold, I asked, "Did you discuss the firing of bullets into the rear of our car?"

"Yes."

"Why?"

"We have to show the Russians that the Stasi shot."

"They know it."

"But they will deny it."

"The Russians in Schwerin saw the back of the car after the incident. Besides, what is the purpose?"

"We have to place the Russians on the defensive."

I was getting more irritated by the minute. "Forget it, and don't discuss any further details with the colonel unless it's about your role in the matter. Remember, I was the responsible officer."

J. hesitated and then said, "I told the colonel that I turned into the Stasi car."

"When?"

"Last night."

"No. I mean *when* did you turn into the Stasi vehicle?"

"On the first collision."

"Why?"

"They were harassing us."

I answered, "We were slipping and sliding so much, it was my impression that their car slid into us. I'm going to stay with my assessment, but you are free to give the colonel your version."

Early on Tuesday morning the chief stopped by my office. "Have you changed your report, fella?"

"If you have a minute I'd like to talk to you about it," I replied.

"Minute, hell! I'm on my way to SERB [the Soviet External Relations Branch] to see Colonel Kozlovsky. Have that report ready for me by twelve noon today. Put in the fact that they bashed you with their car and that they shot at you. That's all, fella."

Col. Ivan Kozlovsky, whom I had sized up during a trip to SERB when I had first arrived in West Berlin, sported an artillery insignia on his uniform. Most of us believed, however, that he was a member of the Soviet military intelligence. Kozlovsky was the most atypical Russian imaginable: handsome, witty, sophisticated, and suave. He and I had had several earlier encounters, the most recent being the "Kennedy for

President" button incident. I had no idea how he would react to this more serious event.

Kozlovsky carried on all conversations in Russian so it was fortunate for me that Fitz was on hand to interpret during the meeting between Kozlovsky and the chief. Fitz had been within earshot when the colonel badgered me about my statement and my friend sympathized with my position. Although he was worried about the chief's insistence on accusing the tails of "bashing" the mission car, and the colonel's stubborn position that the surveillance team had tried to kill me, as the USMLM deputy to the chief, Fitz could give no overt help to me during the meeting. However, upon his return from the meeting with Kozlovsky, Fitz did give me a word-by-word translation of the chief's conversation with Colonel Kozlovsky. "John, keep this, but don't say where you got it," Fitz cautioned me. "You may need this if you get into more serious trouble later on about this shooting."

Lt. Col. Fitzgerald gave his account of the meeting: The chief opened the discussion by saying, "I haven't much time this morning, but I have two related matters to discuss. First, I express my deep concern in reference to the shooting incident by personnel surveilling Commander Fahey and Captain J. [surname deleted] last Saturday. These unidentified civilians fired their pistols at Commander Fahey. Second, to indicate to you my deep concern in reference to this, I would like now to ask that the necessary arrangements be made to discuss this matter with General Voronsov as soon as possible. If today is not convenient for the general, I would be happy to meet with him at any time, but my commander in chief is deeply concerned by this development and I am sure that he will want me to relay to him General Voronsov's reassurances that this will not happen again and that the safety of mission personnel will be guaranteed by the headquarters, Group of Soviet Forces–Germany. As you can understand, such action as firing on my people does not accord to the mission the prestige warranted as a mission and as a part of the United States Army."

Kozlovsky listened carefully and then asked, "What are the details, and are you certain that someone fired?"

"Commander Fahey personally saw one of the identified civilians draw a pistol, three miles east of Witzin. Full details were given to the Schwerin kommandant in the presence of these two individuals. I am prepared to give a complete written report to General Voronsov. Prior to the incident two civilians drove their machine in a reckless manner, twice striking the mission car. They drove in front of the car twice, stopping them. They used profanity and their behavior was typical of the lowest order of a hoodlum. Essentially, that is the question."

"Your version is interesting," Kozlovsky replied, "but you neglect several points. Commander Fahey and Captain J. [surname deleted] were driving at speeds excessive for icy roads. They also failed either to properly control their vehicle or, more likely, deliberately collided with a vehicle of the German police. They refused to stop when signaled by the police. Also, the police did not fire a weapon at Commander Fahey. There was no proof offered at the Schwerin kommandantura that the police shot at Fahey."

"In essence your account is correct, but in every other nation of the world police wear uniforms and identify themselves. At my July 29 meeting with General Voronsov I assured him that we would observe the rules. I also said that I could not accept statements and actions of unidentified civilians. If I do this, it means that any civilian in the German Democratic Republic can stop, harass, or otherwise control our cars. You have suggested that Commander Fahey lied in reference to the pistol. I refuse to accept this implication under any circumstances, for it is not the custom of United States officers to lie in an official report. In Schwerin your officers were cooperative and helpful in every respect, but at no time were they able to prove these civilians who you now tell me were police did not have a pistol. If they were police, as you so indicate, then logically they did in fact have guns, for I have never seen a member of the East German police without a weapon. In other words, I cannot accept this statement that they did not have weapons. Further, I fully accept Fahey's statement that they did fire. Even if every other statement that you made were true, which I doubt, there is still no excuse for firing a weapon, or to engage in profanity, or to use such reckless tactics on roads of ice as you have now shown me."

Kozlovsky countered, "Let's consider the possibility that they drew their weapons. Your officers were proceeding at excessive speed, refused to obey police, and tried to leave the scene. In addition, it seems there are two major contentions here. One is shooting. The other is shooting at Commander Fahey."

"I cannot agree. The act of drawing a pistol is inexcusable, regardless of the circumstances. Apparently only a bullet would give you the proof you require. Again I emphasize that it is not appropriate to discuss minor traffic matters when there is no concrete evidence in reference to violation of traffic regulations. Again, I am completely confident of Fahey's honesty and truthfulness. I will not accept even the least implication that he lies and that the word of these unidentified civilians is accepted over Fahey's. It was not until this minute that these civilians, whom I prefer to call hooligans, were identified as police."

"To whom was it not known that they were police?" Kozlovsky muttered.

The USMLM chief pressed the attack. "I cannot accept the responsibility for allegations of unidentified persons under any circumstances. I am equally sure that your mission in West Germany would feel and demand precisely the same courtesy. Now, to further assist you, today before 1:00 P.M. I will forward to you Commander Fahey's complete statement. I propose that you read it and later this afternoon both you and I see General

Voronsov if he has time. If not, I will see him at the earliest convenient time. I do not wish to create any further incident, but I do wish that this be given the personal attention of General Voronsov and that I can personally express my deep concern about this matter, as well as reassure you and General Voronsov of my very keen desire and determination that the mission will at all times obey legal authorities and traffic rules of the German Democratic Republic."

Kozlovsky retorted, "Well, why didn't Fahey stop?"

"He stopped twice. Would you always stop when unidentified civilians tried to stop you, bump you, rob you, and so forth? My mission officers will always stop when they recognize authority is present. I cannot and will not give any assurances that I personally or that members of my mission will obey or honor any instructions of any unidentified persons who conduct themselves in such an undisciplined manner."

Upon his return from Potsdam the colonel bounced into my Berlin office. "The final report, fella, let me have it."

"Here you are, Colonel."

The chief read every line carefully. Not believing his eyes, he read two portions of the report aloud: "It was Commander Fahey's impression that the collision was caused by the surveillance vehicle, pulling abreast of the mission car," and, concerning the second collision, that "the cars collided sharply and it was Commander Fahey's impression that the surveillance car turned into the USMLM car."

"You didn't change a goddamned thing. Why do you refuse to say that they bashed you?"

"Colonel, from what I know after talking to Captain J. this morning, if I were to change anything I would indicate that Captain J. now states that he banged first into the Stasi vehicle. I'm still not sure that he did, so I'm leaving the statement as is."

The colonel fumed. "Now listen to this!" Then he read slowly: "as the car passed to his right a loud pistol report was heard by both USMLM officers. The civilian surveillance person was approximately fifteen feet from the USMLM car at the time of firing."

"Why didn't you say they shot directly at you? You saw them."

"I saw the Stasi who fired draw his gun. I told Captain J. to duck down. We heard the shots. I didn't see him shoot."

"You know damned well they shot at you."

"I know that he didn't. At fifteen feet no one could miss. He fired over the car to force us to stop."

The colonel motioned me into his office and he began to discuss what the army calls efficiency reports and the navy calls fitness reports. These periodic reviews evaluate an officer's performance and affect his promotional progress and career possibilities. "Play ball on this, fella, and you can write your own efficiency report."

"Sorry, Colonel, that's your responsibility, not mine. As I told you when I arrived, the navy prefers that I don't even see this report before it is filed."

"If you don't change these statements you're going to be sorry, fella."

"I won't lie for any reason, Colonel. You do as you think best."

The chief stormed out of the office with my report as written. That same afternoon the colonel met at the headquarters of the Soviet Forces–Germany with General Yakubovsky's deputy, General Voronsov, who accepted my written report of the shooting incident. To everyone's pleasant surprise the Soviets acted beneficially to us by removing all German surveillance from our reconnaissance tours in East Germany. The tails did not reappear until two months before my scheduled departure from the mission in June 1962. I thought that the favorable outcome of the shooting incident would lessen the chief's animosity toward me, but stormy waters still loomed ahead.

УДОСТОВЕРЕНИЕ ЛИЧНОСТИ № 73/А.

Предъявитель сего кап.2 ранга

Джон А. ФЕЙ

является членом Американской Военной Миссии Связи при Главнокомандующем Группой советских войск в Германии.

Нач. Отдела внешних сношений Штаба Группы советских войск в Германии

полковник (КОЗЛОВСКИЙ)

27 мая 1950 г.

Данные о владельце удостоверения

Должность офицер Миссии

Дата рождения 23 апреля 1923 г.

Национальность американец

Рост 177 см Вес 81 кг

Цвет глаз карие

Цвет волос тёмно-русые

Личная подпись

Действительно по 19 г.

полковник (КОЗЛОВСКИЙ)

Действительно по 19 г.

полковник (КОЗЛОВСКИЙ)

Commander Fahey's Soviet Army identification card
Courtesy of USMLM

Soviet colonel Kozlovsky *(right)*, Soviet lieutenant Zhelanov *(center)*, and unidentified Soviet lieutenant colonel

USMLM backup headquarters in West Berlin

Commander Fahey in dress blue uniform with USMLM patch
Courtesy of USMLM

Right: Stasi tail vehicle. *Second from right:* U.S. Military Liaison Mission vehicle.

Potsdam House *(front view)*

Entrance to Potsdam House grounds

Commander Fahey returns to his vehicle after conversation with Soviet Army doctor.
Courtesy of USMLM

Left to right: Air Force captain John Pendergast, Helen Fitzgerald, Cdr. John Fahey, Lt. Col. Charles Fitzgerald
Courtesy of USMLM

Commander Fahey *(far right)* seated with the French at the queen's birthday ball, Berlin
Courtesy of FMLM

President Kennedy speaks to English language students.
Official U.S. Navy photograph

John Fahey with President John F. Kennedy
Official U.S. Navy photograph

Restriction sign at Rostock ferry dock, posted after Commander Fahey's crossing

East Berlin guard tower

Fahey's photograph of the Wall (taken from a bridge crossing from the American Sector)

Reichstag tower

The Wall around the Brandenburg Gate

Checkpoint Charlie (from helicopter)

East Berlin road obstructions across border from American Sector (from helicopter). Note number of obstacles and tank traps facing east and west.

Soviet marshal Ivan Konev *(left)* and Gen. Bruce Clark
Courtesy of USMLM

USMLM vehicle destroyed by fire during Fahey's final reconnaissance tour
Courtesy of USMLM

"Fireball" vehicle's interior
Courtesy of USMLM

12

Sabotage

The chief of the mission evaluated the performance of assigned army personnel using periodic army efficiency reports and the performance of the sole naval member using navy fitness reports. Air force evaluations, called effectiveness reports, appeared to be under the general control of the USMLM chief, though air force personnel operated independently on their own targets and interests. The USMLM chief did not have the responsibility for submitting air force effectiveness reports. Lt. Col. Clark Baldwin, the acting mission chief before the current chief, wrote two outstanding fitness reports on my performance.

The intelligence reports that I submitted concerning my detentions by the Soviets were accurate and true. I was fair to the Russians and never accused them of abuses. Shortly after assuming command of the USMLM, however, the new colonel expressed minor displeasure with one of my reports, believing, I assumed, that I was soft on the Russians. When the time came for him to write my fitness report, he called me to his office and asked about the words printed directly above the spot where he was to sign the report: Has the officer reported on seen this report? "What do I do here, fella? Check yes or no?"

"Most navy commanding officers check no."

"Are you sure? It's a great report, fella. You are doing a fine job."

"I'm sure, Colonel. The commander in chief, U.S. Naval Forces–Europe, emphasized last week that naval officers are not to see their fitness reports before they are submitted by their superiors."

"Okay, fella. That's all I want! You can be sure, fella, that your outstanding work is reflected in this report."

His comments notwithstanding, it was obvious that my fitness report would not be up to par after our altercation over the shooting incident. After a period of time I wrote to Lieutenant Commander Yates who was then stationed in Washington. I gave Yates written authority to check both my record and the chief's fitness report. Yates wrote back that it was satisfactory but not good. It contained faint praise and several adverse remarks, including "His reticence on occasion conceals stubbornness." After reviewing my entire personnel jacket, Fred Yates found the colonel's report to be the lowest performance evaluation I had received during eighteen years of service.

I was not overjoyed with the news, but decided to keep performing as a licensed spy to the best of my ability. However, a visit to the colonel's office several months after the shooting incident brought the fitness report matter to a head.

"Fella, I called you up here to tell you that your next fitness report will reflect favorably on your outstanding work. Your last trip in the zone was the best damned reconnaissance job I've seen yet. You're doing a bang-up job!"

"Colonel, why tell me this when you just submitted a fitness report on me that is lower than any I have received in my entire career?"

"How do you know? You lied! You told me that you couldn't see the report."

"I couldn't see it before it was placed in my official file, and I was directed to inform you so that you could file a report without outside influence. However, there is a provision in the navy that an officer can see his complete record whenever he desires.

I authorized Commander Yates in Washington to view the report."

The colonel informed me that the report had been influenced to some extent by the shooting incident, and had it not been for that one factor he would have given me an excellent evaluation.

The next storm still lingered on the horizon. The colonel had asked me, in a most peculiar way, to change one of my intelligence reports. He reminded me that two navy fitness reports—one outstanding and one unsatisfactory—still sat on his desk, and he wanted to know which one I preferred that he sign.

I responded, "I will not alter the report."

"You are leaving me no choice."

"Whichever fitness report you sign is your responsibility. The intelligence report stays as written."

A few days later the chief again called me to his office. "Have a seat, fella. You can help me in this matter."

"What's the problem?"

"Sabotage!"

"Sabotage! Who's involved?"

"Barbara!"

"Barbara who?"

"Barbara who? Barbara your wife."

Shocked by his words, I couldn't answer.

"Check into it, fella, and lend me a hand with this."

I recovered some of my senses and asked in what way my wife was involved in sabotage. The colonel answered vaguely, "I'm not sure myself yet, but I'm investigating it."

"Who brought this to your intention?"

"The 513th."

Stunned that a charge of sabotage had been made against my wife by the army's counterintelligence corps stationed in West Berlin, I fought for time to think by weakly replying, "I'll look into it, Colonel."

The chief was not ready to let me go. "I am completely neutral in the matter. I cannot accept the information as true, but on the other hand I cannot accept the information as false. Either way it is a clear case of sabotage. Although I can't believe that your wife is responsible, I cannot accept either that she is guiltless. When I find out, someone will be nailed good."

My wits began to return. The chief was groping for a way to get to me, and he had found it through my wife. At the first opportunity I excused myself from the conversation and headed home. Shortly after our conversation the colonel appeared at my house. (Barbara describes his visit and her subsequent actions in her book, *Berlin Wall Flower.*) Finally I telephoned the commander in chief, U.S. Navy–Europe representative in Frankfurt, West Germany, and explained the entire scenario. Capt. Ross Hirshfeld assured me that he would investigate the charges at headquarters in London and then come to Berlin.

A day after my call navy captain Hirshfeld informed me that he would confront the mission chief on the following day, and asked me to meet him and a second naval officer at the Berlin Dahlem Station. After driving the two officers to the Harnack House (the officers' guest residence in West Berlin), I called on the colonel to make a two o'clock appointment.

"Here, fella! They're in Berlin. What for?"

"They came from Frankfurt to investigate the sabotage."

"God Almighty, when did they come?"

"They arrived on the morning train."

"Christ, I was on the same train. I could have briefed them about the whole affair myself."

"Naturally they want me to be present, Colonel. They don't need Barbara. Anyone that you desire to invite that has any contributing information of course would be agreeable to the captain. Will fourteen hundred be convenient, Colonel?"

"Yes. God Almighty, they're here in Berlin. I can't believe it."

We arrived at the chief's office at two o'clock sharp. The chief was alone and greeted us with the utmost courtesy. He began by praising my work in the Soviet Zone, calling me his "ace in the hole."

"Not as deep as he wished," I mused to myself.

The naval officers listened politely, and then Hirshfeld said, "Of course we are glad to hear this, Colonel, but as you know, we are here on more unpleasant matters. What is the present problem involving Mrs. Fahey?"

The colonel paled noticeably, then replied, "This has been a relatively minor problem, but now very recently has been cleared up. We don't need to go into it anymore."

The captain responded, "But I'm informed that it was a case of sabotage. Is this true?" Despite my past worries, I found myself hoping now that the chief would respond by saying "yes." Had he denied the charge and continued to make light of the incident, I would have had no proof that he had pursued us so relentlessly.

"It was not sabotage, but alleged sabotage. I was able to nurture the tree of truth, kill the seed of doubt, and now Mrs. Fahey is not guilty and you will be glad to hear, John, not even suspected."

Then Captain Hirshfeld commented, "Don't you think sabotage is a rather strong term to use without, apparently, any basis at all?"

"There were grounds for sabotage. There is more to this. I have been neutral. Now I can nail someone. Not Barbara, of course."

"Who involved Barbara?"

"They asked me not to reveal names. You know the 513th. Sources are not released. However, I can assure you that Barbara is not guilty."

Hirshfeld concluded the discussion with the hope that no unpleasantness would arise, and said, "John has expressed his satisfaction with this assignment. You have indicated your high regard for his work here. I hope that he will be able to perform his assignments without further harassment about sabotage or any other interference."

The colonel smiled broadly to me. "Fella, you know how much I have appreciated your work here. Unfortunately, Captain, John was not too happy with a fitness report that I gave him, but as I told him, I intended it to be an excellent one. You must be patient with me. I'm just not used to navy ways."

"Well, Colonel, you won't have to worry about this any more. Admiral Smith in London will write John's fitness reports from now on. Of course, I'm sure that he would be pleased to receive your comments from time to time concerning John's performance."

The colonel was disturbed. "You understand that I would not have the slightest objection, but I don't feel that Heidelberg would go along with this. It is a matter of proper channels. Of course I will talk to CINCUSAEUR and let you know later."

To my surprise the captain responded with, "No need, Colonel. I called Heidelberg on the phone this morning and CINCUSAEUR agrees. Earlier I spoke with Admiral Smith, CINCUSNAVEUR, in London, who is sending a letter to Heidelberg on the subject. By the way, Admiral Smith will be visiting you in the near future. I hope that you can give him an inside look at your mission."

The chief rose up on his toes with apparent eagerness to welcome the admiral to his unit, and then slid over to my side, placed his arm around my shoulder, and said, "We'll show him around. Won't we, fella?"

"You wouldn't send me off to Guestrow, would you, Colonel?"

Understanding my reference to my hastily prepared trip with Captain J. during the air force inspection visit, the chief replied,

"I like a sense of humor in my officers. This is a little private joke, Captain."

My wife suffered the most during this terrible siege, but together we survived this most recent unpleasantness with the colonel. I was able to concentrate on my assignment without further difficulty. On many subsequent reconnaissance trips the chief rode with me. He always drove the mission vehicle and let me run the tour. I worked with Lt. Col. Fitzgerald on all high-level meetings and often interpreted in Fitz's place when the chief met with the Soviets. The chief's comments to London were always positive. When my assignment at the USMLM ended I was one of only two officers recommended by the colonel for a Legion of Merit. When Colonel Fitzgerald was transferred to the Army War College in Kansas, the chief asked if I would extend my USMLM duty assignment to be his deputy chief. I declined.

13

Navy Targets

During my first eight months at the USMLM the navy required no intelligence collection of any kind from me, though of my own volition I did photograph Soviet vessels, an East German shipyard, radar installations, and communication stations and sent intelligence reports to Washington. The Office of Naval Intelligence gave little or no response to those reports.

Ninety-five percent of my reconnaissance trips were to collect intelligence for the army (though the Office of Naval Intelligence did receive the evaluations of my reports and photos). During these army trips, with few exceptions, I wore an army uniform. At times my army colleagues even offered to collect navy information for me, but since I had been given no direction from my navy superiors to do so, I had no specific tasks for them to accomplish.

Finally, after serving eight months at the USMLM, out of the blue I received a requirement from the U.S. Navy, one of only two that I received in over two years at the mission: the navy wanted a telephone book from the northern coastal area of the Soviet Zone. I faced a real challenge. Surveilling the Soviet Army, photographing field maneuvers, or riding surreptitiously on Soviet military trains were child's play compared to acquiring an East German telephone book. Even ordinary East

German citizens didn't have their own copies. The only books I could locate were resting in local communications centers that handled mail and housed telephone and telegraph offices. Telephone books—one to a center—were chained to the wall in an entryway that was perpetually packed with regular people looking for numbers from the single available book.

The request sat on my desk for a couple of weeks. Though I was having no success at getting the book I hadn't given up, but simply put the navy's request low on my priority list. It did bother me a bit that I was neglecting the only request the navy had given me so far. Three weeks passed before army captain Bill Schneider stopped by my office in Berlin, informing me that he was going to the north and wondered if he could do anything for me while he was there. In passing I mentioned the East German telephone book, though I was more interested in hearing about Bill's recent attempt to drive a Soviet tank back to Berlin.

A few nights earlier Bill had found a broken down and temporarily abandoned Russian T-54 tank near Potsdam. Bill had gotten in and tried to get it started for the trip to West Berlin. Although he didn't succeed in driving the tank out of the Soviet Zone, Bill did bring back a lot of valuable information. My efforts to acquire a telephone book seemed minuscule in comparison.

A few days after Bill returned from his trip to the north I ran into him at the West Berlin headquarters.

"Got a minute, John? I've got something for you."

"Sure, Bill."

Bill returned in a couple of minutes with an East German telephone book with an attached chain dangling almost to the floor. "Where did you get it?"

"In Wismar."

"How did you get it?"

"I couldn't get the chain off the book, so I just ripped the other end from the wall. I hope it's what you want."

I looked at the telephone book. It covered a large area in northern East Germany. "It's perfect. I owe you more than one for this." It took two army soldiers at Berlin headquarters to remove the heavy chain for me without damaging the book. I was happy to have fulfilled, through Bill's aggressive action, the navy's sole requirement of me, and sent the book to the Office of Naval Intelligence in Washington. I never flinched while standing in the middle of a road, photographing oncoming Soviet tanks, but ripping a telephone book chained to the wall in a crowded communication center in East Germany was beyond my chutzpah.

During the cold war the East Germans called the body of water to the north of Germany the Ost See ("East Sea," in English). Because it is to the west of Russia, the Russians use a different name: the Baltic Sea. (Now that it sports attractive resort hotels, present-day Germans call the body of water and adjacent shores a Baltic paradise.) Each year in July the East Germans staged a small fair commemorating Ost See Week on a fairgrounds west of the city of Rostock. The industrial, agricultural, and nautical fair attracted me as an interested spectator and as an intelligence photographer because I was the only American naval officer in East Germany, and because the fair always featured several communist-originated nautical innovations.

In July 1961 Deputy Chief Fitzgerald and our driver, Sgt. Dick Keezer, accompanied me on my annual trek to the fair. The Russians had posted a sign along Route 105 near the coast prohibiting liaison mission members' entry into the fairgrounds, but no similar sign was posted along the road that approached the fairgrounds from the west. In addition, the entire area north of Route 105 was marked as restricted on maps provided to the USMLM by the Soviet Army. Yet, since the line on the map was drawn just to the north of Route 105, I always claimed that a sliver of unrestricted territory to the north of the road was "open." The fairgrounds were on the north side of Route 105.

We approached the fairgrounds from the west. The open tract of land near the highway that was used for parking was six to twelve inches deep in watery mud, and we were not dressed in our field clothes. Fitz voiced his reservations about having to wallow in the mud to get to the main building but Keezer wasn't so reticent. He immediately said, "I'm staying in the car."

Fitz acquiesced and together we waded in mud up to our ankles all the way to the main attraction area. We wandered around the exhibits independently, and I used one of our three Leica cameras to photograph a number of nautical displays. The most interesting invention I saw was a new shipboard radar antenna. I photographed it from every angle and then took close-up shots with a zoom lens. The surrounding crowd grumbled a little about my obvious interest in the antenna. Since there were few naval targets available in East Germany and since most of my activities centered on U.S. Army military intelligence objectives, I took advantage of every opportunity to bring back good photos of the navy and merchant marine displays.

After an hour and a half I rejoined Fitz, who was obviously enjoying our time away from the usual pressures of reconnaissance tours. "I found an interesting apparatus," he said. "It automatically cleans and shines shoes."

"Great," I replied, looking at my mud-covered shoes. "I've never needed a shoe shine more than now."

Fitz pointed to the machine. I placed my entire foot in the thingamajig and pressed a button. A whirling action of some sort began inside the machine. "This machine might give me an excellent shine, Fitz, but what a racket! It sounds like a turbine in a hydroelectric plant. Hey, Fitz, my foot is beginning to feel hot."

Fitz smiled, "It must be done. Pull it out."

I pulled my foot from the contraption. With utter disbelief we stared at what little remained of my shoe. Half the leather had been skimmed off the top of the toe. "Another sacrifice to the cause, Fitz. These were not old shoes."

"Well, did you get everything you wanted here, John?"

"I'm real pleased, Fitz. Let's go." We sloshed through the mud back to our vehicle. As we arrived at the staff car, we were confronted by a Russian colonel standing in front of the car. His boots were submerged in the slime. I asked Keezer how long he had been standing there.

"He has been there for about half an hour."

The Soviet looked to be about five feet tall, but in the mud he was closer to four-feet-six-inches. I greeted the Soviet with a friendly "Hello," to which he shouted, "You were photographing in there!"

"That's right, Colonel. I always take pictures. Why are you here?"

"I was called on the telephone. A complaint was registered with the police, charging you with photographing."

"And then the police called you? Well, what's the problem?"

"You were photographing."

"You told me that, and I told you that I know it."

"You can't photograph."

"Why? I always take pictures. If I couldn't photograph, I wouldn't even come here. Do you think that I would live over here for your food, hotels, or shoe shines? Now, do you have anything further, because if not, we intend to leave."

"You are in a restricted area!"

"Colonel, you are new here. Did you replace Colonel Saigada as kommandant?"

There was no acknowledgment from the colonel about his present status, so I continued: "Colonel, the restriction line on our map is north of the road. We are in a little space between the line and the road. We aren't restricted from this place. I visit every year."

The colonel seemed to be sinking deeper into the mud as he answered, "You are on a road with a 'no passage for foreign military mission personnel' sign."

"We came from the west. There is no sign preventing our entry from that direction." I never ceased to be amazed at the immunity we claimed by proceeding on these roads in a direction opposite to the face of a sign that prohibited passage to foreign military missions in English, French, German, and Russian. We were always coming out from behind prohibition signs. Why the Russians failed to place a sign on the other end of a sensitive area was always a mystery to me.

The Soviet colonel again reversed his line of questioning: "You were photographing."

"Colonel, what more can I say to you? You have repeated this charge many times. I do not deny photographing. I always do this. Tell your superiors to have me removed from the headquarters of your commander in chief if you object to me photographing. Now move aside or I am going to register a formal complaint to my chief about you for detaining me without justifiable cause."

Fitz and I got into our car. The Soviet colonel remained in front of the bumper, apparently digesting my words and weighing the possibilities of actions he could take. Then, almost impulsively, he stepped aside. I told the driver to turn slowly and drive by him. As we passed by the Soviet colonel, mud splashed on his pants.

"He must be really new, Fitz. He never asked for identification. He doesn't even know who we are. Our license plates are covered with mud. He doesn't know whether we are Americans, French, or British. I hope that he thinks that we are Brits. I seem to be able to get Brits in trouble with the Soviets without the Brits knowing I am the culprit behind their problems. Maybe it's the Irish in me."

Fitz replied, "I recall that you were detained last summer up here by Colonel Saigada for entering a restricted area."

"This short colonel must have replaced Saigada. Since he didn't ask for our documents and doesn't know our names, I decided not to ask him his name and in turn remind him to ask for ours."

On the road to Stralsund we laughed about the naivete displayed by the Soviet colonel. "Saigada would have held us for at least three hours for back talk like that," I remarked. "The new ones never know how to act because each time they are seeing an American for the first time."

About three hours later we reached the outskirts of Stralsund. At the city limits we were flagged down by a Soviet captain, standing beside a GAZ-69.

"Why are you stopping us, Captain?"

"The kommandant wants to see you. Follow me."

"Not until you tell me why."

"I don't know why."

"You flagged me down and are detaining me and you don't know why?"

"I know why. I stopped you because my kommandant ordered me to stop you. Now get into your vehicle and follow me."

The captain convinced me that he was more versed in this kind of exchange than the Rostock colonel, so I complied and followed him to the kommandantura. Inside the old brick building the local kommandant, a lieutenant colonel, took our identification cards and gave them to the duty officer. I pressed him for the reason for the detention and he answered, "You were traveling with four in the car and now have three."

"This is not true. The three of us left Potsdam. We never had four in the car."

"You left Rostock three hours ago with four, but you dropped one off between here and Rostock."

"Who reported such a lie?" I fumed.

"Someone telephoned."

"Who was it? This happens quite frequently in East Germany. Someone is always calling to report that we are traveling with four in the car instead of three, or three in the car instead of two."

"I don't know who it was."

"Perhaps it is the same person making these calls all over the Soviet Zone. Last week this happened in Halle. It seems to me that the Soviet Army could track down this individual."

"Well, I don't know who it was."

"Then you are detaining us on the basis of an anonymous phone call. Where did the call come from?"

"From Rostock."

"Then how could the caller say we dropped someone off between here and Rostock?"

"I don't know."

"Isn't this poor Russian efficiency?"

"The Rostock duty officer from the kommandantura called," the lieutenant colonel finally admitted.

"*Aha!* Now this Rostock kommandant himself knows that we had three in the car and not four when we left Rostock, because we talked with him. I would like to remind you of a wise Russian saying that the state wants good Soviet citizens to live by."

"Which one?"

"The bitter truth is better than a sweet lie."

"I am just doing my duty," answered the lieutenant colonel, returning our documents to us. "You can go."

Sergeant Keezer had stayed in the car, as was our usual practice. "What was that all about?" he asked when we returned.

Fitz answered, "I think that the lieutenant colonel was called by the Rostock kommandant, to have him report our names. Without our names he couldn't write a report. Picking us up on any trumped-up charge was the easiest way to check our passes and learn our names."

I added, "Usually they don't let the arrested individual take the offensive like the lieutenant colonel did, but I think he was embarrassed by the situation the more-senior Rostock kommandant had put him in. I wish that I had remembered that 'bitter truth' proverb when I was detained by Saigada last summer. He got the best of me during an exchange about the truth."

While inside the kommandantura I had noticed that some of the officers and men standing nearby were enjoying our verbal exchanges. A major smiled several times when the lieutenant colonel fumbled for an answer. No one was hostile. I turned to Fitz. "After splashing mud on the Rostock kommandant, I don't plan to be around that area for a while, but Stralsund looks promising. Our army reconnaissance teams rarely travel in the extreme north, but the British and U.S. Air Force teams cover the area on occasion. Fitz, do you want to come up here again?"

"I wouldn't mind, but I think that I'll stick to the large Leipzig fairs. I'll never get the mud off these shoes."

"Fitz, pity the Rostock kommandant with mud on his trousers and no commercial cleaners."

The photographs from the fair, taken without a flash, were excellent. I forwarded them to Washington in an intelligence report. I threw away the muddy shoes.

14

Entry onto Mystery Island

On an earlier overnight stay at the city of Stralsund's Baltic Hotel, we were forced to remove the room's door at 3:00 A.M. to exit the hotel. The USMLM had issued a peculiar device with a key that could be inserted into an old-fashioned keyhole to block someone on the other side from unlocking the door. When slipped into the keyhole, a turn of the key forced flanges in the device to spring out; when the key was withdrawn the device stayed securely fixed in the lock.

Almost all East German hotels had "peek through" keyhole locks. I felt safe when we slept with the device in place because no one could then quietly pounce on us. Though the "key blocker" had worked for me several times without a problem, on this occasion when I inserted the key into the device to retrieve the flanges it wouldn't turn. We couldn't unlock the door from inside the room, and we were trapped until I realized that we could take the door off its hinges. The driver and I managed to remove the door with the gadget still embedded in the lock. We leaned the door against an inside wall of the room and tiptoed out of the hotel. Needless to say, when I returned to that hotel for another visit I was apprehensive about the reception I might receive. To my surprise the desk clerk made no mention of my previous faux pas and the driver and I checked in without difficulty.

Rarely did mission officers make courtesy calls to the local Soviet kommandantura while overnighting in a city, but this time I decided to make such a visit. My planned itinerary was accomplished and I had not slept in a bed for three days. I was exhausted. Once in a while a local Soviet kommandant would rouse mission officers in the middle of the night to force them to register at the kommandantura if they had failed to appear at his office before getting to their hotel. I decided this time to take no chances, pay a call at the kommandantura, and retire for a good night's sleep.

Having been escorted to the kommandantura during our recent detention after the Rostock fair, I was confident that I could direct Keezer to the office's location. However, in the dark the desolate area was unfamiliar. After a few wrong turns down some blind alleys we found the odd-looking structure—which resembled the Bates Hotel in the movie *Psycho*—at the end of a dirt road.

No lights were visible either outside or inside the building. I left Keezer in the car and approached the front door. There was no bell and the door was unlocked. I entered quietly. To my right was a room with a large glass window and a dim lamp that lighted the surface of a cluttered desk. I moved around the outside corner of the room into a pitch black corridor. I felt for a door and eventually found a knob, but the door was locked. So much for a collection opportunity!

The building appeared empty. I groped my way along the hall and finally noticed a sliver of light coming from a cracked open door. I thought of returning to the building's front entrance, but feared I might encounter a Soviet who wouldn't spend a moment asking why an American was coming out from deep inside this Soviet military administrative headquarters. I crept up to the door and listened. I heard several voices and sharp banging noises. I decided to burst into the room and tell the occupants that I had been unable to find anyone at the entrance. I abruptly flung the door open and was hit in the face with several small flying objects. In defense I closed my eyes. When I opened them I was surprised to see dominoes scattered on the floor around me. The Soviet officers and soldiers had been playing dominoes. My sudden, unexpected entry had startled a player near the door, who in a reflex action had flung his small missiles into my face. Everyone in the room was stunned by my appearance.

"Who are you?" asked a major.

"Please excuse me. I am staying at the Baltic Hotel tonight and I am making a courtesy call on your kommandant."

"Who are you?"

"An American officer who was detained here some time ago. There was no one at the front area and I have been searching for someone on duty."

"Sit down. Join us. We weren't expecting visitors."

"Thanks. I am sorry to have disturbed all of you."

"Not at all. We are glad to meet you. None of us have been to America. Comrade Khrushchev made a long visit to America over a year ago. How did the American people like him?"

"He had a successful visit to the cities, farms, Hollywood, the White House, and Camp David. I helped translate the script into Russian of an American submarine's first voyage under the ice at the North Pole. President Eisenhower and Khrushchev sat together and viewed the film."

"Did Comrade Khrushchev behave himself?"

"Better than usual. He didn't pound his shoes on the table this time."

"What! When did he do that?"

"During an earlier visit at the United Nations."

"My God! That's our Nikita Sergeevich!"

From then on Khrushchev was referred to by his first name and patronymic. The Russians were eager for a long continued dialogue, but I was weary.

"I left my driver in our car and should leave."

"Can you come back and chat again some time?"

"Sure."

"Can we do anything for you?"

"I don't think so. I've tried to get permission to go on to Ruegen Island, but there is a sign at the entrance to the bridge, prohibiting entry. I asked Colonel Kozlovsky in Potsdam for permission, but have had no success."

"Why do you want to go to Ruegen Island?"

"Don't be fooled by this army uniform. I am an American naval officer. I would like to go to the city of Sassnitz on Ruegen where there is some naval activity."

"Kozlovsky doesn't give orders around here. Can you wear your naval uniform?"

"Yes."

"Come up here in your naval uniform. Ask for me, Major Ivanov. I'll get you on Ruegen Island."

"I'll be back next week. Many thanks." I thought, "What do you know. I've got Soviet friends in Stralsund who will get me onto the mystery island."

Ruegen Island, the largest and most beautiful of the German islands, is accessible by land only across a drawbridge from the city of Stralsund. During most of the cold war the island was strictly off limits to all foreign liaison missions. An entry prohibition sign was placed on the Stralsund side of the bridge. The brigadiers who headed the British Military Liaison Mission in the early 1950s took a keen interest in Ruegen Island and, according to the account by Tony Geraghty in *Beyond the Front Line,* British brigadier Dewhurst sought permission from the Soviet kommandant in Stralsund to visit the island. The kommandant refused Dewhurst's request to enter Ruegen but, with typical British determination, the brigadier drove to the bridge. The bridge was blocked by three Soviet officers and twelve Stasi hoods. Three Stasi vehicles attempted to tail Brigadier Dewhurst back to Potsdam. Later, in 1952, Royal Marine major Reynolds outfoxed the Soviets and did succeed in entering Ruegen Island (with a long detention as his reward).

The island attracted interest because of its mysterious past under Hitler and the secrecy later imposed by post–World War II restrictions. Hitler chose Prora, a small city adjacent to the seaside resort of Binz, to build a fantastic complex of buildings that stretched two-and-a-half miles along the Baltic beach. A rail line was constructed to transport to the resort paradise the expected throngs of the German privileged class. Hitler conceived of the complex as a "Kraft durch Freude," or holiday vacation spot for twenty thousand people. It was not completed before World War II began, and during the war the construction work on the enormous complex stopped. The Allies' firebombing of Hamburg in 1945 led the city to relocate those left homeless to the massive Prora housing development. During the cold war various German army units occupied the site. Today Prora touts its railroad museum, which houses at least twenty locomotives.

During my tenure at the USMLM the army members there showed no interest in Ruegen Island, mainly because the Soviet Army was their main intelligence target. The Germans possessed antiquated military equipment, including old World War II Soviet T-34 tanks. So, aside from interest in German anti-aircraft missile bases, the staff at the USMLM paid no heed to the East German military. In addition I had little opportunity for collecting naval intelligence information anyway. The port town of Sassnitz on Ruegen Island offered the best chance to find the Soviet and German navies. Meeting a Soviet major in the Stralsund kommandantura offered a stroke of good luck: I was to get authorized entry onto Ruegen Island.

On my next trip to Stralsund I headed for the kommandantura. Soviet major Ivanov greeted me warmly and said, "You want to go to Ruegen Island."

"Yes, but there still is a sign at the bridge prohibiting passage."

"Don't worry about the sign. Arrive at the bridge one half hour from now and you can enter the island."

"Thanks, I owe you."

"You owe me nothing. The army should not prevent the navy from getting to the sea." We said our good-byes and the driver and I made our way to the bridge. A dozen police, positioned at the bridge's entrance, blocked our entry onto the drawbridge. Ten years earlier Brigadier Dewhurst had been refused permission to cross, had tried to cross anyway, and was prevented by a similar number of people. Now I had secured permission to cross from a Soviet authority, but nevertheless was being barred from entry to the island.

We returned to the kommandantura. The major seemed surprised to see me again. "Did you go to the bridge?"

"Yes, but it was blocked by German police. Someone must have told them we were coming. Also, I am driving a Mercedes today with an American flag on the license plate."

"I called them, requesting that they not interfere with your passage. Go back there again. I assure you that they will not stop you."

Back again we drove. Not a single vopo was at the bridge. We crossed and drove the thirty miles to Sassnitz. We found an outstanding view of the harbor from a street on a hilltop near the waterfront. I didn't even have to leave the vicinity of the car. I sighted and quickly photographed about half a dozen Soviet minesweepers and three new Soviet torpedo boats. I was tempted to drive to Prora eight-and-a-half miles down the coast to the south, but decided to head back to Stralsund. Halfway back we met a convoy of six police cars speeding in the opposite direction. The driver asked, "Where are they going?"

"They're after us. They let us on the island, but they don't plan to let us travel alone without company. I'm glad that I photographed what I wanted and we left Sassnitz."

During the rest of my tour of duty at USMLM I periodically repeated that same scenario: race to Sassnitz, photograph the naval activity, return immediately to Stralsund. On almost every visit to Ruegen I met a convoy of police cars before getting off the island. No other USMLM officer had ever been allowed on Ruegen Island. Ruegen remained a mystery island even to me, to whom the Soviets had permitted entry. But I was privy to everything going on in the Sassnitz harbor, my primary quest.

Another mystery was the number of "perks" that I received from the Soviet Army. The Soviets caught me many times after I had retreated from prohibited missile bases and airfields. General Voronsov accepted my account of the Stasi shooting incident without reservation of any kind. General Yakubovsky always singled me out with warm greetings. Yet any one of these indiscretions could have led to my being given persona non grata status and being removed from USMLM.

The Soviets created good personality profiles on every USMLM officer. They knew that I pursued my assignments with conscientious zeal, but did not assume an attitude of going to war with them every day. Also, my support of Kennedy in the U.S. presidential election may have paved the way for all Stasi tails to desist for over a year, that is, until the Soviets learned that I was being transferred out of USMLM.

The Soviets knew that I supported the election of John F. Kennedy, and eight months after I arrived at the mission he was elected. Down in the dungeons of the West Berlin mission headquarters, protected by bars and combination locks, a photograph taken of John Kennedy and me sat on my desk. The Soviets knew it was there. Perhaps someone reported it to them. The mission employed a Russian native speaker who assisted USMLM officers in improving language proficiency. He did not have authorized entry to this allegedly secure basement, but on one occasion when I had left lunch early I did find an unauthorized Brit perusing American "eyes only" classified documents that were lying on the USMLM operations officer's desk. In the spy profession one cannot be sure of friends or of the absolute security of supposedly protected spaces.

Entry onto Ruegen was a special accommodation to me. I was grateful but gave nothing in return. The next time I visited Stralsund I was surprised to see that the sign prohibiting passage to Ruegen Island was no longer posted at the foot of the bridge.

15

Berlin Wall Crisis

The decision to erect the Berlin Wall was not a spur-of-the-moment, impulsive initiative by the Soviets or the East Germans. The evacuation of East German factory workers, doctors and other professionals, and farmers from the countryside had steadily increased over many months' time. In the summer of 1961 drastic measures to stop the exodus were imminent.

Tightening the Noose around Berlin

At 3:00 A.M. on Sunday morning, 6 August 1961, while I was reconnoitering in East Germany near the northern border of West Berlin, an East German border guard accused me of being a "dirty spy." That morning we had already encountered an unusual number of grepos on every road and trail leading to the city because, despite an effort to seal the two-hundred-mile perimeter of Berlin, more than three thousand refugees from all regions of East Germany had passed into East Berlin and then crossed over to West Berlin over the weekend.

These weekend defections meant that on Monday mornings East German factories and plants were forced to operate with few key supervisors and essential workers. Fall harvesters were plagued with manpower shortages, and as a result it had been impossible to gather all the crops on collective farms. The prospects for the coming harvest season were even gloomier. Every facet of German life had been affected by the flight of people, and the entire industrial complex faced a shutdown.

On the previous two weekends in late July the East German police had established checkpoints at the entrances to all autobahns leading into Berlin. In addition, on 28 July special police checkpoints had been established on all secondary roads within fifteen miles of Berlin.

Increasingly drastic measures taken each successive weekend before the erection of the Wall on 13 August had failed to stem the tide of fleeing East Germans. Yet the magnitude of the exodus demanded immediate action. More than six hundred thousand refugees were flown out of West Berlin during the five-and-a-half years before the Wall was erected. Between the fall of 1960 and the building of the Wall, more than one hundred thousand people had taken advantage of the open border between the Berlins to escape to the West.

Because the July efforts to discourage car travel to Berlin had failed to decrease the number of defections, the first secretaries of the communist parties of all Warsaw Pact nations were summoned to attend meetings held in Moscow on 3 to 5 August 1961. There the secretaries decided to close West Berlin completely. Since the eighty-eight-mile border between East Germany and West Berlin was already barricaded, by erecting physical barriers along the remaining twenty-eight-mile border between East and West Berlin the encirclement of West Berlin would be complete.

The East Germans were assigned the task of building a physical barrier between the Berlins, while the provision of the necessary military support fell to the Soviet Army. Participants in the Moscow meetings selected the night of 12-13 August to reveal the operation's fait accompli to Allied commanders and Berliners when they awoke on Sunday morning. Positioning a preponderance of Soviet forces, including an overwhelming number of tanks, was essential for precluding any possible ground counteraction by Western military forces stationed in Berlin. The territory selected for this strong military support was along the East German–West Berlin border in favorable tactical positions for a ground attack into West Berlin from the north and south. On the west side of West Berlin the Havel River prevented disposition of Soviet troops and tanks.

To minimize the expected Western outcry the Wall was built at least three meters inside the East Berlin border. To make a dramatic show of strength and resolve the Soviets reactivated Marshal Ivan Konev, a First Ukrainian Front commander and World War II hero of the final drive to Berlin. Marshal Konev assumed command of the Group of Soviet Forces–Germany, after replacing Gen. Ivan Yakubovsky, who stepped down to be Konev's deputy. Konev, the last active Soviet officer who had been a close associate of Joseph Stalin, was a rival of Marshal Georgi Zhukov during World War II. Stalin had even taunted Konev into beating Zhukov in the race to Berlin. Marshal Konev also was the chief justice of Lavrenti Beria's trial. (The notorious Beria, who had been Stalin's right-hand man in the bloody purges and terrors in the thirties, was chief of the NKVD, the predecessor of the KGB. Beria was executed immediately after Chief Justice Konev found him guilty.)

Upon Konev's arrival as the new commander in chief, Soviet Forces–Germany, an invitation to meet him at a small reception was sent to a few of us at the USMLM. During the reception I made a point of addressing him by his first name and patronymic: Ivan Stepanovich. Other Americans, awed by his presence, sought his autograph and addressed him as "marshal." In 1961 Konev was sixty-four years old and seemed to me much like a "granddaddy." However, I did notice an obvious sign of fear among the other Soviet officers present. None of them wanted to get anywhere near Konev. I tried to entice one or two to join me in conversation with Konev, but they pleaded with me not to drag them in. (This fear of Konev was something that I could and did use later in another circumstance.)

The Russians and Germans had one week to plan, coordinate with military backup, and carry out the detailed steps of constructing a physical barrier on the East Berlin–West Berlin border. Many signals were given that the West anticipated the coming Soviet action. USMLM officers reported seeing visible evidence of the tightening of the noose around Berlin. A new Soviet hero had taken command. Western commanders and the majority of Berliners had retired for a peaceful night's sleep on Saturday night, 12 August 1961. But the U.S., French, and British Liaison Missions were wide awake and on watch, waiting for the last twist of the noose.

The Night of 12–13 August 1961

The first sign of action was the movement of Soviet tanks from their installations in Potsdam, Nauen, and Krampnitz (a military installation between Potsdam and Nauen) to the border of West Berlin. Once the tanks were in place the Germans began stringing barbed wire between the Berlins.

The USMLM was the first to detect tank movements. Whenever tanks moved along the hard surface road a quarter to a half-mile from our Potsdam House, vibrations shook the walls. The deafening roar of the rumbling tanks as they turned and moved along the Potsdam Road could be heard ten miles away. The sound was almost enough to wake the dead.

Air force lieutenant Nick Yankowsky and driver Mel Ratz were in the Potsdam mission house when the tank movement began. They drove to the end of the road that connected the house to the main road. At the intersection they were stopped by a dozen Russian troops, who proceeded to throw a tarpaulin over the mission car. Every time Mel raised his hand toward the gearshift the Russians raised their AK-47s to firing position. Through a tiny slit in the tarp Mel could see all the tanks and guns moving south.

After an hour passed the tarp was removed and Mel and Nick were permitted to return to the Potsdam House.

Though Nick was new to mission operations, Mel Ratz was an old hand at it. Mel suggested trying to drive on a back road north through the Potsdam House's garden to the hardtop road toward Nauen. Mel's idea was a good one because they soon found themselves among a convoy of tanks, guns, troops, and military vehicles leaving Krampnitz and heading south. Mel even managed to drive past a few of the vehicles before being forced to stay in line. When Mel and Nick reached a pontoon bridge that Soviet engineers had erected across a river, the Soviet traffic regulator actually signaled the USMLM vehicle to cross with the Soviet tanks. Mel and Nick recorded the final disposition of every tank.

Finally the occupants of a Stasi car sighted them. Mel struck the Stasi vehicle a couple of times in the rear. In the confusion the Russians let the USMLM car leave and tried to detain the Stasi vehicle. Mel and Nick returned to the Potsdam House with their report. Later other mission officers raced to follow other tanks to their destinations. Soviet military vehicles banged, bumped, and pushed our vehicles aside as the Russian convoys proceeded to various locations along the West Berlin border. Despite the harassment and great efforts by the Soviets to prevent observation, the USMLM teams were able to track the Soviet units to each chosen disposition point along the border.

At the moment the tanks left their sheds I was asleep in West Berlin. The telephone rang about 1:00 A.M. The summons to get a mission car and proceed immediately to Potsdam was not unusual. Telephone calls to USMLM personnel were as effective as fire alarms are to firemen, and seldom did any mission officers get a full night's sleep. By the time I arrived in Potsdam driving car no. 11 (the only USMLM Mercedes), the tanks had taken up positions on the West Berlin border and were ready to roll into West Berlin. As I drove around on some of the roads that the tanks had taken to the border I saw hundreds of tank tracks on severely damaged roads north, west, and south of the West Berlin border.

Shortly after dawn on 13 August I drove one of the most damaged mission cars back to West Berlin for repairs. Already hundreds of West Berliners had gathered on the Berlin side of the Glienicke Bridge across from Potsdam. Upon seeing the muddy and damaged U.S. vehicle the crowd cheered.

Obstructions were already in place between the Berlins. Actually the structure later referred to as the Wall, which in some places rose fifteen feet high and was ten feet thick, was built over a period of a year. In the early days the original fence was frequently crashed through during escape attempts and even blew down during a wind storm.

The Wall closed seventy-six streets, five railroad lines, and four underground metro lines. It interrupted the daily trips (going both directions) of about five hundred thousand people. Thirteen control points were established when the Wall was erected, but later the communists reduced this number to seven, including Checkpoint Charlie. (Checkpoint A [Alpha] was located between East and West Germany, near Helmstedt; Checkpoint B [Bravo] was between East Germany and West Berlin; Checkpoint C [Charlie] was between East Berlin and West Berlin.)

Most of the publicity about confrontations between East and West described threats and minor skirmishes between East and West Berlin. The real danger came from the north and south of West Berlin, far from the Wall that separated the Berlins. Had a real conflict arisen, hundreds of Soviet tanks would have moved into West Berlin. The fewer than twenty operational American tanks located in West Berlin would have provided no significant opposition.

The Wall was in place. Soviet tanks were disposed on the East German side of West Berlin. Nothing further occurred during the several days following Sunday, 13 August. Every day

USMLM personnel checked the positions of the Soviet tanks. No change. Everyone was waiting to see who would take the next step. It was President Kennedy's move.

Kennedy's Response

President John F. Kennedy's options were severely limited. Not willing to risk confrontation with the Soviets but eager to bolster the morale of West Berliners, Kennedy sent Vice President Lyndon Johnson to Berlin on 19 August. The next day, a Sunday, a U.S. battle group traveled from its home base in West Germany across the one-hundred-ten-mile Soviet Zone to West Berlin.

Concerned about Soviet reaction to the addition of a battle group to the Western armed forces already stationed in Berlin, and to lessen the chance that the Soviet Army would be able to prevent entry or harass this force while en route, Western leaders for the first time provided a complete written manifest of the convoy's composition to the Soviet border control at Helmstedt. (Unfortunately this courtesy created setbacks in later access questions because the Soviets then demanded written manifests for all subsequent U.S. military convoys to Berlin.)

On Sunday, 20 August, I was dispatched to the woods along the one-hundred-ten-mile Helmstedt autobahn to observe the convoy's passage through the Soviet Zone. I was instructed to inform authorities in West Berlin of any attempts to stop or otherwise interfere with the army's movement. I found an excellent observation point next to the autobahn about ten miles east of Helmstedt and waited, waited, waited. For over an hour and fifteen minutes beyond the designated time of the convoy's passage not a single military vehicle moved on the autobahn. I had no radio or other means for contacting Berlin. If the convoy encountered any difficulties en route I was supposed to race back to Berlin and sound the alarm like Paul Revere. I knew that once the convoy arrived at Helmstedt any complications would be handled and reported by the Americans at the checkpoint; it was the area past the checkpoint where my responsibilities began. Finally after ninety minutes of anxious waiting I saw the convoy approach. Later I learned that the convoy had delayed its arrival by making a wrong turn in West Germany. In the lead was the battle group commander, Colonel Johns, standing proudly straight as a ramrod though he had no clue that just a few feet away, from the edge of the woods, a fellow American was admiring his military carriage. I tracked the convoy by following trails near the road, sometimes concealed by trees only three feet from the U.S. tanks as they rumbled toward West Berlin.

The Soviets took no action to interfere with the American convoy. Sending an additional battle group to the most untenable military garrison in the world, where tanks numbering in the tens were surrounded by Soviet tanks in the thousands, exerted no threatening pressure on the Soviet Union. The U.S. action appeared to be a warning to the Soviet Union and East Germany not to take additional steps and also to prevent West Berliners' morale from sagging under the Soviet threat.

Soviet historians reveled in learning of former West German chancellor Konrad Adenauer's chagrin about the Americans' "fear before the Russians." To President Kennedy's credit, his unwillingness to take more decisive action was prudent thinking. Thousands of operationally ready Soviet tanks poised on the western border of West Berlin held a margin of superiority unprecedented in military confrontations. A decision to fight the Soviet Army in this situation would have made Custer's last stand appear insignificant.

The Soviets gave several signals that no further steps were planned unless a meaningful Western response was taken. The Wall was erected inside the East Berlin border. Other obstacles prevented aggression by either side on the border between the Berlins. Tank traps faced to the east as well as to the west.

Sending both the vice president and a battle group to Berlin a week after the Wall's erection convinced the Soviets that the West contemplated no significant serious opposition. Although the Soviets kept their tanks on the West Berlin border until late fall, Soviet officers were particularly calm, friendly, and unconcerned during September and October.

All returning USMLM reconnaissance tours during the fall of 1961 included a circling of Berlin to check on the status of the Soviet positions along the border. On occasion I found troop reinforcements. Only once did I observe an active exercise taking place. The exercise looked threatening and dangerous since, for the first time, it appeared that the Russians and Germans were training together. However, after blundering into an East German command post, being detained and then turned over to the Russians, I found the Soviet military thoughts and intentions far from ominous.

When Soviet units returned to their home bases, Mel Ratz again was on the job. Mel's alertness to the importance of intelligence collection matched that of any USMLM officer. USMLM patrols were dispatched to identify every Soviet unit returning from the West Berlin border. Mel was alone in the Potsdam House when he heard the Krampnitz regiment returning to the north through Neu Fahrland. He walked to the bus stop on the west side of the main road and watched all of the Soviet units passing, recording the side numbers of every tank and vehicle.

Later, when Mel joined the other officers who were comparing their findings, they discovered that only Mel had observed and collected information on the Krampnitz tank regiment. Later the USMLM chief vented his anger at Mel for having left the Potsdam House unattended while he went to gather his information. Hardly a single USMLM officer would have done differently.

With the return of all of the Soviet forces to their home bases, as far as the Russians were concerned the Berlin crisis was over. New recruits began to arrive for the new training cycle that began on 1 December.

Wall of Shame

The USMLM had no interest in East Berlin before or after the erection of the Berlin Wall. The main intelligence target of members of the USMLM continued to be the Soviet Army and Air Force. The only significant Soviet military unit stationed in East Berlin provided the honor guard at the Soviet World War II Memorial in West Berlin. The Soviets always bitterly regretted that two prominent sites—the War Memorial and the Reichstag—were located not in the Russian but rather in the British sector of Berlin.

During my off-duty hours I explored both West and East Berlin. Before the erection of the Wall one could enter and leave East Berlin on any of the seventy-six streets that connected the divided city. Not all streets between the sectors had signs identifying the border, so I relied on the police uniforms I saw to know where I was when I crossed the boundary. During my first year at the Potsdam mission I became very familiar with both cities. After the Wall went up, on my off-duty days I tried to approach different sections of the Wall from the East Berlin side, always to be rebuffed by the East German Grepos. I sometimes even found myself between the guards and the Wall, a dangerous position to be in: the many escape attempts, some of which were successful, had made the guards edgy and prone to shoot rather than ask questions.

Since my duties in East Germany gave me enough danger and excitement to last a lifetime, I often decided to take my leisure walks along the city's boundary, photographing the Wall from the west side. From time to time for almost a year in 1961 and 1962 these strolls were a welcomed and relaxing diversion from my stressful liaison and operational trips in East Germany. At first strolling along the Wall fascinated me, but soon I became eager to view it from a higher elevation. The top of the Reichstag offered an excellent platform—the old parliament building that was still a burned-out shell in 1961 was located near the Brandenburg Gate almost flush against the Wall. Unfortunately there were no staircases leading to the top and the building was under British control.

With a little effort I was able to persuade British authorities to permit me to climb to the top of the southeast tower. The only way up was by extension ladders, a difficult feat when encumbered by a camera and telephoto lenses. The top of the building towered over the Brandenburg Gate in East Berlin. I shot some excellent photographs of the Wall and the area surrounding the Gate, including Hitler's bunker located a short distance east of the Wall.

East German border guards gazed with puzzled faces at the solitary figure hanging over the top edge of the Reichstag, aiming a long black tube in their direction far below. From only a few visits I was able to obtain detailed photographs of the thick wall erected in front of the historic gate. The climb to the top of the Reichstag seemed more precarious each time so I was greatly relieved to have completed the task.

Learning of my favorite pastime, a U.S. Air Force friend and neighbor who was stationed in West Berlin offered to help me photograph the Wall from a helicopter. My friend, Romey, served in a West Berlin intelligence unit. Earlier in the year he had asked for my help in finding a sample of the Soviet chaff (finely cut strips of foil or fiber dropped from Soviet aircraft in East Germany that are disseminated in the air in cloud forms to reflect energy and conceal air force flight formations from radar detection). Romey advised me that the most likely and easiest places to find chaff would be in puddles after a rainstorm. He was right and was delighted when I collected samplings of chaff on some of my reconnaissance trips. Romey's unexpected payback for this personal contribution to his intelligence reports was making air force helicopters available to me when I was in West Berlin.

On some days a small helicopter would land near my house. On other days I would go to Tempelhof Airport to catch a ride on a larger helicopter. The smaller craft was handy, but the larger one permitted photographing through the side door, open and clear of Plexiglas.

The helicopter pilots were less than enthusiastic about flying directly over the Wall, but I was usually able to persuade them that we would not encounter any problems. Every flight came with a barrage of questions: "We're not over the Wall, are we? We haven't crossed over yet, have we?" We flew low in order to stay on the west side of the Wall, which often zigzagged in ten-meter increments. To their questions I always answered, "We're okay," even when looking down through a powerful telephoto lens directly into the eyes of a startled East German grepo.

The view of the Wall from the air revealed several surprises. The many obstacles that were arranged on the east side were visible in minute detail, showing that movement on the roads in any direction was impossible. Embedded tank traps prevented Soviet or East German tanks from crossing into West Berlin and Western tanks from crossing into East Berlin. A more complex array of barricades was established on roads leading to the American sector of Berlin, possibly indicating a greater concern about U.S. reaction to the Wall's construction. Later scrutiny of one photograph taken of an unusual gathering of border guards near the Wall in Potsdamer Platz—a town square inside the British sector where the three western sectors joined—revealed what appeared to be the fatal conclusion of an attempted escape that had taken place just minutes before we passed over the scene.

Except for witnessing the occasional tragedy, the helicopter flights were a welcomed relief from the eighty to ninety mile per hour automobile chases, sideswipes, crashes, and shootings that routinely occurred during our reconnaissance tours of East Germany. Two trips were terminated by totally demolished cars, two by hospitalizations for injuries received, and two from shooting incidents. I found strolling alongside the Wall or flying over it to be great fun and a chance to enjoy a lull in the hectic schedule of direct encounters and confrontations with Soviets and East Germans.

One flight especially highlighted for me the different values held by the West and the East. When the Wall was erected, the British placed barbed wire around the Soviet war memorial in West Berlin, thus depriving the Soviets of a continued opportunity to lure the large crowds of visitors who frequented the site. The detachment of Soviet soldiers who guarded the memorial was still admitted by the British. From the helicopter platform I noted that without visitors to the memorial, the honor guard no longer stood watch as they had when tourists were present, but instead loitered around smoking. I couldn't imagine such behavior by the honor guard at the tombs of the unknown soldiers in Arlington National Cemetery.

Since my photograph of the Soviet honor guard with their AK-47 guns at the memorial in the days before the Wall was built garnered a first place award in the 1962 All Navy Photography Contest, I should express my gratitude for the Soviet honor guards' performance. Yet to me the Wall always remained a "Wall of Shame."

Romey was a good friend, but I doubt that he would have succeeded in arranging personal helicopter flights over the Wall for me had I not gathered the chaff in the Soviet Zone. Ironically a huge clump of Soviet chaff as large as a softball later fell from the sky into Romey's own West Berlin backyard.

Russian Fears

On the Soviet side the Berlin crisis ended before 1 December 1961 when the Group of Soviet Forces–East Germany began its annual training cycle. Operating a boot camp for new recruits was a primary function of all Soviet armies. A multitude of shaved heads appeared every December. No exception was offered to the vanguard Soviet military force that faced NATO armies across the German border. The Russian troops went into winter hibernation as basic instruction transpired inside warm classrooms. On the Western side the Berlin crisis had not ended. President Kennedy activated the reserves and continued to ship reinforcements and supplies into Europe, continuing the buildup into the winter months of the new year.

While Soviet leadership was unconcerned about any possible Western military response in the immediate area of Berlin, it did have a growing fear about Western reaction to the crisis on the continent. All global Soviet military initiatives took place in late summer or fall when the Soviet Army was at the height of readiness. Soviet apprehension about President Kennedy's reinforcement of NATO was the major topic at a 23 February 1962 holiday celebration in Frankfurt, West Germany. At the USMLM's kindred mission, the Soviet Military Liaison Mission in Frankfurt, West Germany, fourteen Soviet military personnel enjoyed the same privilege of free travel in West Germany as we, their American military counterparts, did in East Germany. Unexpectedly, my spouse, Barbara, and I received an invitation from the Soviet mission in Frankfurt: "The Chief of the Soviet Military Liaison Mission to the Commander in Chief, U.S. Army–Europe, Colonel and Mrs. M. I. Chernikov, invite Commander John A. Fahey and wife to a reception in honor of the 43rd Anniversary of the Soviet Army and Navy to be held at the Soviet Mission on 23 February 1962 from 1800 to 2000 hours."

I knew little about the Soviet Mission in West Germany. Under the Huebner-Malinin Agreement the host command structures provided food for their missions. On one occasion the Soviet members complained about being able to receive only frozen meat from American suppliers (as compared to the meat provided to USMLM by the Soviets, which was fresh but also full of worms and other unidentified creatures). When I learned of this Soviet grievance, I suggested that we send our contaminated but fresh meat to the Soviet mission in Frankfurt. The recommendation ended the matter and Western frozen meat continued to be acceptable.

We were greeted warmly upon our arrival at the Soviet mission. The toasts began at 6:01 P.M. and continued one after another. The effect of ice cold vodka (which of course had to be drunk "to the bottom" each time) was offset to a degree by the large quantity of food Barbara was able to cram into my mouth between toasts. During the evening every Soviet officer present asked me to carry a message to President Kennedy, emphasizing that the crisis had been over for months. When I pleaded ignorance about the reinforcements arriving every day in Europe, the officers began to describe in detail what they had been observing at various ports and airfields. Over and over the message was, "We don't want war. The crisis ended months ago. Please tell your president."

As the evening progressed the toasts continued and the pleas to inform President Kennedy intensified. I couldn't avoid "chug-a-lugging" drink for drink with the Russians. Thanks to Barbara's attentiveness, though, I was more sober than others.

At 8:00 we were at the door to leave when the last appeals for peace and friendship were made with three additional toasts. I staggered down the steps somewhat aware that one more toast would have finished me off. The Russians had finally got me drunk, and at the same time had hammered home their obvious fear about Kennedy's final reaction to the Berlin crisis.

16

Marcantonio's Bambinos

After the Berlin Wall was built every reconnaissance trip in the Soviet Zone was followed by a circling of the outside boundary of Berlin. At 1:00 A.M. one Sunday that fall I was beginning my pass around the city when I came up behind a Soviet convoy proceeding to the north. I decided that we needed to overtake the convoy to check its composition and number of vehicles, but, like all secondary roads in East Germany, the two-lane road we were on was bordered by gigantic trees on both sides. If a vehicle approached in the opposite direction a head-on collision was a certain result.

Joining us on this trip was Maj. Henry Marcantonio, one of the many backup army and air force personnel in West Berlin who had never traveled in the Soviet Zone. Marc was being relieved of his assignment as adjutant of the USMLM. To give him one last opportunity to travel in East Germany before his departure, the Soviets issued him a temporary pass. I escorted him on his first and last ride in the zone.

When we began to pass the convoy I asked Marc to count the vehicles and the driver to concentrate solely on the road, while I identified the composition of the convoy. Marc began, "One, two, three . . . Do we really want to do this? Suppose a car is approaching in the opposite direction."

"That's the rub. The chances after midnight are less than 10 percent, especially if this convoy is not too long."

It was long. When we passed the forty-first vehicle I, too, began to worry, even though by this time the driver had increased our speed to about 65 mph. Marc's voice, calm at first, rose to a loud and obviously tense level. I was quiet but dying inside. I would have preferred to face some angry armed Soviet or German soldiers than run a convoy at night on a lonely dark road. The seventy-seventh and last vehicle was a GAZ-69, and I breathed a heavy sigh of relief. We were finally passing the front of the column. The driver was silent, but Marc wasn't too happy with my judgment. He commented, "You could have killed us. Why not just follow them to their destination?"

The drivers were always good about following the decisions of the tour officers in charge, and never questioned an action even when they were sure that they would have acted otherwise. I tried to explain to Marc that I ran all convoys and then laid in wait to follow them. It was the only way that I knew to be sure to make a worthwhile and accurate intelligence report. I chanced having a head-on collision every day. I didn't like running convoys, but it was part of the job. I didn't have time to convince Marc of that, who was sure a better way could be found because suddenly we had a mass of humanity ahead of us on the road. The driver veered to the right into a open field and brought the car to a stop in front of an open-sided tent. There were hundreds of Germans wearing helmets all around us. Marc was now speechless, but the driver asked, "What are you going to do, Commander?"

"I am going to get out and say 'Good evening' even if it's morning." I walked around among the East German soldiers and said, "Good evening." To my surprise all of them replied pleasantly with the same greeting. It was about five minutes before a German officer approached. He was puzzled about our presence and told me that this was Command Post Number 28. I told him that I was associated with the Russian army when he said, "Here come your comrades now."

The lead GAZ-69 drove close to us and a Soviet senior lieutenant in the vehicle asked the German, "Are we ready?"

"You have some visitors here."

The Soviet turned to me. "Who are you? Identification, please." I handed him my identification and he headed for his radio. After making a call he returned with instructions for us to remain exactly where we were until a representative from the Oranienburg kommandantura arrived. Twenty minutes had passed when the angriest Soviet officer I had ever seen arrived on the scene. He literally screamed, "Return to your car! Get in! Stay in! And then follow me!"

All the way to Oranienburg Marc voiced his concerns: "We are in real trouble. We will never be released. For the first time East Germans and Russians have been observed in a joint operation. They are planning an attack across the border into West Berlin. They'll never let us get back to report this. We've had it!"

The driver was silent. I told Marc that every day in East Germany is an adventure. Running a convoy on a narrow road is a life-threatening event, but detentions are sometimes fun and challenging. "There are only two outcomes: They will declare me persona non grata and kick me out or warn me and let me stay. My goal is to get a stiff warning. If not, so be it."

Marc was not convinced. "This time you've seen too much. They will never let any of us go."

"Marc, you have never been over here before. Don't bet on it!"

At the kommandantura the major ordered me out of the car and barked at his driver to guard my driver and Captain Marcantonio. Marc was not to leave the vehicle. The major then escorted me physically into the building. Without the usual wait before interrogations began, the major directed me to take a seat at a table with him, a Soviet captain, and a junior lieutenant. I looked at my watch. It was 2:30 A.M. "You have committed a serious offense: espionage. You were in a disposition of Soviet troops!"

"Major, I have a question."

"I ask the questions, but go ahead."

"Why do I always see majors during arrests, sometimes colonels, but never a single podpolkovnik [the equivalent of lieutenant colonel]?"

"From now on I ask the questions. You have been arrested before?"

"Many times."

"Well, this time in the disposition of military troops. I read your identification which forbids this. Do you deny it?"

"No. As soon as I cross into the Soviet Zone I am in a disposition of Soviet troops. Twenty-two divisions."

The major refused to acknowledge my response. "I have read the back of your identification card. You are forbidden to be in the disposition of military troops. Do you deny that you were arrested at command post 28 of the German Democratic Republic Army?"

"I do not deny that I was detained, but we do not recognize the German Democratic Republic Army. There is no international legal basis for such an organization."

"Soviet forces were also present. You have been caught spying. We are writing up a protocol for your signature."

"I sign no protocols. You are wasting your time."

"Let me assure you, you will not be released until you sign the protocol." This major meant business. Efforts to engage him in small talk failed. He was the most focused Soviet officer I had ever encountered. I was beginning to tire when a slightly inebriated Soviet colonel entered the room.

The colonel slurred a few words, "What and who do we have here?"

The major reported, "A spy caught early this morning at German Army command post 28."

"What kind of a spy?"

"An American."

"An American? A capitalist American? Are you a capitalist?"

Now the tables were turning on the major. The colonel had taken charge. I directed my responses to the Soviet: "I am an American, but hardly could be called a capitalist. My father was a worker."

"A worker? Your country exploits workers. You couldn't be an officer if your father was a worker. Our officers are the sons of workers, not yours."

"Colonel, I think that you have a nineteenth-century view of America, when we had 'robber barons' in America."

The major sat silently, beginning to fidget and showing signs of exasperation. He tried once to interrupt by interjecting mention of the spying matter, but the colonel continued to direct his comments and questions to me. "Robber barons, you call them. Who were they?"

"The Rockefellers and other industrial giants who used their initiative and know-how to build up American industry and railroads. Now in twentieth-century America the immigrants who worked for them are enjoying economic and political freedoms never before realized in any country in the world."

"Political freedoms? How can your country compare with the motherland of Marx, Engels, and Lenin."

I added, "And Stalin."

"Thank you. Yes and our great patriotic war generalissimo and hero of the Soviet Union, Stalin."

"Colonel, I am glad that you admire Stalin, who worked so closely with our President Roosevelt in pursuing the German Nazi beast to his den and annihilating him. I was saddened when your leaders removed Stalin's body from beside Lenin in the mausoleum and buried him along the Wall."

The colonel smiled. "You talk our language. What is your name?"

The major grabbed my identification card from the table, but the colonel looked to me for the answer. Now was the time to give my first name and patronymic in Russian: "Ivan Ivanovich."

The colonel responded, "Ivan Ivanovich, my name is Gerasim Nikolaevich." There was no question in my mind about with whom I was dealing. Obviously the colonel was a political officer while the major was a line officer. The major had lost control of the interrogation to a tipsy colonel who was more interested in political banter than in my serious violation of the Huebner-Malinin Agreement. For the first time since we began our run past the Soviet convoy, I relaxed.

"Colonel, I'm sure that we have the same likes and dislikes."

"What would that be?"

"Well, I would bet that we have the same favorite American presidents." Most Russian officers knew the names of only a few American presidents. My World War II Soviet peers usually chose Roosevelt as their favorite (because of his lend lease aid) but always with some reservations about the Western delay in establishing a second front. The young ones already liked Kennedy. But there was only one logical choice for a Soviet political officer.

The colonel took the bait. "Who would I like?"

"Lincoln!"

"You do know me. Lincoln freed your slaves. We honor him in our 'Abraham Lincoln Brigades.' We even have some Abraham Lincoln Brigades in your country. As a son of a worker, you must favor him also."

"Gerasim Nikolaevich, we have our favorites. He is my choice." Had I taken a lie detector test right at that moment I would have passed with flying colors. Throughout my childhood my mother had extolled the many admirable characteristics of Abraham Lincoln. Every story of his honesty was repeated on an almost daily basis. The poor major was now completely out of the picture. "Gerasim, I told you about the many immigrants who made America what it is today. We have Russians, Greeks, Jews, Irish, and countless others who now play a large role in our great country. Sitting in my vehicle waiting for me is a son of an Italian immigrant. Would you give me permission to go to the car and bring him in to meet you?"

"Please, bring him in here."

I left the building alone and went to my impatient and anxious colleagues.

"Marc, come with me. A Soviet colonel wants to meet you."

"Commander, are they going to kill us?"

"You don't know the Russians, Marc. I have only one request. Don't sing 'O Sole Mio' inside."

"Stop kidding. We are in real trouble."

I returned to the room with Marc. The major was pleading the case against us, but the colonel was paying no attention. The colonel turned to Marc and in Russian said, "You're a friend of Ivan Ivanovich."

I interpreted. Marc then asked in English, "Do they understand English? Who the hell is Ivan Ivanovich?"

"I don't think either knows a word of English. I am Ivan Ivanovich."

"What about our transgression?"

"The angry major is out of it. The colonel is a little drunk and a new friend. Tell him about your Italian heritage and your family." Marc, nervously at first, jabbered about his origins in Brooklyn, his parents, and then a long dissertation about his immediate family. The colonel showed some interest, but his attention began to wane until Marc mentioned his children.

"You have children in America?"

"In West Berlin."

"What do these Italian children look like?"

Mark took out his wallet and unfolded a bevy of photographs of his young babies. He said, "They are American, but I call them my 'bambinos.' "

The colonel turned to me. "Ivan Ivanovich, explain for me, bambinos."

"It's a diminutive of 'bambo' which means child or baby, Gerasim. I believe that it is of Italian origin."

The colonel started to giggle. "I like it. It sounds Russian. My daughter has two bambinos."

"What are their names?"

"Sasha and Maga."

"Beautiful names!"

"Are you ready to go, Ivan Ivanovich?"

"To leave, Colonel? Yes."

"Well, now you are in a restricted area where our kommandantura is located. The area where you were arrested is not restricted, but the major will have to escort you to the border of this restricted area and set you free. You will ride in our vehicle with the major. Your vehicle will follow. Outside the boundary you will transfer to your vehicle."

We shook hands with Gerasim Nikolaevich and departed. On the fifteen-minute ride with the major he refused to speak with me. When I got out of the vehicle I said, "Many thanks, Major, for the ride."

His only response was, "It was my duty," expressed in Russian by one word, "sluzhba." We arrived at Berlin mission headquarters at 5:30 A.M. At the debriefing Marc expressed his belief that an invasion of West Berlin was imminent since the Russians and Germans were seen coordinating their troop actions for the first time. I disagreed with Marc's assessment. I found the Germans in the command post area calm and friendly and lacking the hostility needed to begin an attack. There was no sign in the Soviet kommandantura of anger, excepting on the part of the Soviet major who was just trying to do his job. The only significant intelligence we gained was the knowledge that the German and Russian armies were coordinating their training exercises, possibly in the event of a confrontation if the Berlin crisis deteriorated. This training and coordination of the two armies should have been expected.

Whether an experienced army officer's opinion was to be believed over the opinion of a naval officer with some knowledge of the Russians was of little concern to me. "Let me get to bed before I am called again on this quiet Sunday to cross into East Germany on another reconnaissance tour. Marc, give my love to the bambinos!"

17

It's Not a Truck

The trip began on a quiet Saturday morning in the fall of 1961. Everything had remained fairly calm on both sides after the Wall had been erected, until dependents of Soviet officers began fleeing across East Germany into Poland. Military trucks carrying women and children had been sighted on the autobahn headed toward Frankfurt across from the Polish border. The commander in chief, U.S. Army–Europe directed the USMLM to count the number of Soviet women traveling to Frankfurt on a typical Saturday and turned the assignment over to me. I convinced air force lieutenant Nick Yankowsky to drive the mission vehicle.

My orders were to stay on the autobahn near the Oder River between Berlin and Frankfurt to gather an accurate count of the number of trucks and Soviet dependents that passed by from dawn to dusk. I looked forward to the assignment, mainly because it would give me an opportunity to get to know Lieutenant Yankowsky better. Nick had arrived at the mission just before the Berlin Wall crisis. Despite tremendous harassment on the night of 12-13 August, Lieutenant Yankowsky and Mel Ratz had tracked the Soviet tanks to the border of West Berlin. It was a rare occasion for an air force officer to be involved in an army mission. Maj. Matt Warren, chief of the USMLM's air team, forbade the use of any of his air force personnel on army trips and never permitted army members to join air force reconnaissance tours. Nick Yankowsky obviously volunteered for the Saturday mission without Matt Warren's knowledge.

All day we drove back and forth on the sixty-mile portion of the east-west autobahn. Throughout the day I counted half a dozen flatbed military trucks with a total of 120 women and children as passengers. Having nothing with which to compare the number of departures, I had no idea whether or not the pullout from East Germany of 120 women and children was significant and cause for alarm. Both of us felt sorry for the poor passengers packed into the backs of the trucks. The Soviet Army usually transported the wives and children of army and air force officers in this way. I am sure for their part they gladly suffered this hardship in exchange for the opportunity to live abroad. Soviet enlisted men were not permitted to have their families join them while they were on active duty, nor were they permitted to fraternize with local inhabitants.

I photographed the departing truckloads. Far more intriguing to me, however, was the number of Soviet trucks traveling on the autobahn carrying military equipment that was unfamiliar to me, including two sophisticated radar antennas. Nick would slow beside the Soviet trucks which gave me time to photograph their military contents from every possible angle. Sometimes an entire week passed without a single sighting of Soviet military equipment. On this particular Saturday everything was being handed to me "on a silver platter" and I was thoroughly enjoying myself. After all, I wasn't trudging through the woods in army field clothes, hoping to get close enough to photograph the intricacies of Soviet equipment with a powerful telephoto lens. I was dressed in my navy uniform, riding in comfort, taking photographs of objects only a few feet away.

When darkness arrived we headed back to the Potsdam mission house by leaving the east-west autobahn and driving north on the uncompleted road on the west side of Potsdam. I leaned down in the front seat to store my camera and lenses in their cases. As I snapped the covers on the lenses I felt our vehicle accelerate. Though the German autobahns have no posted speed limit, we had been traveling about 60 mph. I looked up to see the gigantic lighted barrier blocking the two lanes on our side of the autobahn, a warning that the second bridge across the river had not been restored after World War II. The bridge that served traffic coming in the opposite direction was intact, so northbound traffic was shifted across to the southbound lanes for two-way traffic across the bridge.

I shouted to Nick, "It's not a truck!"

In the seconds available I tried to warn Nick of the Überfahrt (that is, the crossover) but it was too late. We were only a few feet from crashing through the barrier at 70 mph and plunging into the river below. Nick immediately hit the brakes and turned the steering wheel fully to the left. The wheels dug into the grass island and the car, one of the new 1957 Chevrolets provided to the USMLM in the 1960s, began to roll. The car struck the ground on my side, forcing the roof to the bottom of the right seat and squeezing me to the rear of the car. Had I been wearing a seat belt my head, shoulders, and upper body would have been crushed.

When the vehicle settled upside down, I was lying on the rear window with a trickle of gasoline dripping onto my face. I hollered to Nick, "Are you all right?"

"Yes."

"Did you turn off the ignition?"

"No."

"Turn it off."

I struggled to crawl out the left rear door window. Nick looked to be completely trapped inside. The metal roof that once had been above my head formed a wall on his right side. His head never struck the top of the enclosure around him, which resembled a tepee. Surprisingly, it took only a few minutes to slip Nick out of the vehicle. My head and left elbow had struck the overhead when the car rolled, but I felt fine. Nick said that he was not hurt.

I had never felt so vulnerable in the Soviet Zone. Standing in the dark with no means of transportation or other means of communication, we were easy prey for both the Stasi and the Soviet military. My first thought was to rid myself of the three rolls of film I had taken during the day. I found the cameras in the wreckage, removed the film, walked down to the river's edge, and reluctantly buried the film in the soft sand. Regardless of the seriousness of many past detentions, I usually kept film on my person without fearing that my supposed immunity would be violated. Alone and in the dark without a clue of the outcome of events, however, I did not want to risk compromising my status as a USMLM officer. Carrying evidence that I had been photographing military objects was far more damaging than facing a report that someone had seen me taking pictures. I regretted losing the film, but under the circumstances I believe that choosing to dispose of it was the right decision to make.

Thirty minutes after the accident a motorcyclist approached the scene. The rider seemed unfriendly and unsympathetic, so I did not give him the telephone number of Potsdam House. I said to Nick, "We may be in real trouble. He will probably call the German police."

An hour later a car stopped about ninety feet from the upside-down wreck. Two adults slowly approached the car. Surprised to see me as they neared the locale, the man asked in German, "How many are dead?"

"No one," I replied.

"I can't believe it. There are no dead?"

"We are not even injured, but need your help."

"What can I do?"

"Go to the first available telephone and call number 308. Please tell whoever answers where we are and that we need immediate help."

"We have our children in our car and are afraid to stop anywhere until we get home. I am willing to telephone from my home."

"Where do you live?"

"About 50 kilometers from here, in Oranienburg."

"I would be most grateful if you will do this as quickly as you can." The German family left. I estimated that help should arrive about an hour later. During the next seventy minutes there was only silence. The uncompleted autobahn was seldom used.

The darkness and silence were broken by headlights and vehicles approaching simultaneously from the north and from the south. The two vehicles from the south carried German police. The vehicle from the north was a USMLM car. I was overjoyed to see air force major Matt Warren, the feistiest officer in the mission. Warren asked, "What happened?"

"We had an accident and overturned."

"I can see that. Who was driving, Commander?"

Nick responded, "I was."

Matt growled, "You're through."

There was no time for further discussion. The East German police began to shout, "All of you leave! The car and its contents are in our hands now."

Matt, Nick, and Mel Ratz stood in front of the damaged car. I replied, "You better call the Russians because it will be their decision."

One of the East German policemen went to his car radio. Matt said, "We can push this car over onto its wheels."

I could barely believe my eyes as everyone pushed the car on its side and then back upright on its wheels. It was then that I noticed some blood on my uniform and soon I began to feel badly. Until then I had been feeling fine because I had been in shock.

The impasse came to an end when at 11:00 P.M. a Soviet lieutenant arrived. He was drunk. He slurred the information: "I am the traffic safety officer on duty."

"We want to return this car to Berlin."

"I'll inspect it." The lieutenant squeezed into the metal "tent," pressed the brake pedal and said, "Passed. You can go."

The German police went into a frenzy. Matt said, "Sorry, fellows. The Russian traffic safety authority has made the decision. Mel, get in and we'll push you to Berlin." By now I was feeling poorly and I was happy to let Matt take over. The police were still screaming as we left. It seemed to take forever to reach the checkpoint at Glienicke Bridge. We left the wreck there, on the West Berlin side. Mel dropped Matt off at the Berlin mission headquarters and drove me to the Berlin army hospital.

Upon arrival at the hospital there was a long discussion about where to put me. Finally, at 2:30 A.M on Sunday morning, I was placed in a large room. After fifteen minutes two orderlies entered the room and one said, "We've got to move you."

I was hurting so badly now, I didn't care. I found out later that this spacious well-appointed room was reserved for the U.S. commander of Berlin, kept vacant at all times in the event that he became sick. I soon learned no other rooms were available because my bed was jammed into a supply closet. I asked for something to relieve the pain, but was told I had to wait until a doctor saw me.

About 8:00 A.M. Barbara was called and she rushed to the hospital. By now I was a sorry sight, bruised head to toe. When she stood at the foot of the bed and found me crammed into a closet she was indeed an "unhappy camper." She asked if I had been x-rayed. When I told her that a doctor had not yet examined me, she left to contact our USMLM chief. Thirty minutes later I was wheeled out of the closet to get an X ray, and then moved to a hospital room (not the general's). A doctor told me that I had had a concussion, as well as an injury to my back and left arm. I was hospitalized for several days and then scheduled for therapy.

From time to time several different USMLM army officers exchanged accreditation status among themselves, but as the only navy member I had a permanent pass to the Soviet Zone at all times, unless I was on leave. Because of the time I needed to recover from my accident injuries, I had to surrender my pass to travel in East Germany for six weeks.

I tried to minimize Lieutenant Yankowsky's responsibility for the accident—I was to blame for not alerting him about the lighted barrier. At the time he had been a mission member for only a few months and was unfamiliar with the road hazards. But Major Warren was adamant about following through on Yankowsky's transfer from USMLM. I regretted Nick's departure. He was a good officer and had the potential to be one of the best reconnaissance officers at the mission. I understand that his service record was temporarily besmirched by the incident, but later it was restored.

Certain phrases associated with events in the Soviet Zone will never leave my memory. At the top of the list is, "It's not a truck!"

18

A Sad Thanksgiving Day

A U.S. Army night train left West Berlin every night to cross the Soviet Zone to West Germany. When the train reached the West Berlin–East Germany border, the locomotive was unhooked and the West German engine and engineer were replaced by an East German engine and engineer. As the army train traveled through the Soviet Zone it had immunity as U.S. territory (except for the engine). Upon its arrival at the East Germany–West Germany border after the 110-mile journey across the Soviet Zone, the situation was reversed: the East German engine was replaced by a West German one. The train's commander was usually a U.S. Army lieutenant. As it did not recognize the German Democratic Republic, the United States held the Soviet Union responsible for the train's passage through the Soviet Zone.

On Wednesday evening, 22 November 1961, one of these U.S. Army trains departed West Berlin, packed full with military personnel and their dependents, all looking forward to the beginning of a short Thanksgiving vacation in West Germany. When the train reached the East Germany–West Berlin border it was hitched to an East German locomotive then run by an East German engineer. During the train's passage through the Soviet Zone it slowed to round a bend. At that moment the engineer happened to look back toward the inside arc of the curve and saw a young East German boy jump onto the train. The boy disappeared into one of the cars. The engineer immediately stopped the train at Marienborn and summoned East German authorities. East German police arrived at the scene and demanded custody of the young boy reported by the engineer to have leaped onto the train.

The train's commander, a U.S. army lieutenant, declined to release the boy to the East Germans. The East Germans and East German engineer refused to permit the train to continue through the zone until the boy was given up to them. The train commander maintained that the young boy was now protected by the United States since he had entered a territory of the United States (a U.S. military train) with immunity. The two sides had reached an impasse. This standoff continued throughout the night and into the next Thanksgiving Day morning. (Three years later a Hollywood film titled "Stop Train 349, starring Jose Ferrer and Sean Flynn, was produced about this incident. The movie did not portray events accurately.)

I was in West Berlin at 11:30 A.M. on 23 November 1961, preparing to enjoy a quiet Thanksgiving Day dinner at the Harnack Officer's Club. Our family had just sat down at the table when I was called to the phone. It was the USMLM chief.

"Fella, get down here to the Berlin mission, fast. We've got a problem."

"Okay, Colonel. I was just getting ready to have Thanksgiving dinner with my family. Shall I tell Barbara to go ahead without me or will I be able to return shortly?"

"Get here pronto, fella! Forget your Thanksgiving dinner." I sped to the West Berlin mission house. The chief and Lieutenant Colonel Fitzgerald were waiting.

"This is the situation, fella. The army train was stopped last night and is sitting in the zone. We've got a trainload of passengers spending Thanksgiving on the train in East Germany. A

German boy jumped onto the train last night. The train commander won't give him up. Fitzgerald and I are going to the site and you will be the liaison between the Berlin commander, General Watson, and the Soviet external relations branch in Potsdam. If we do not hear from you or the Soviets, we will overrule the train commander and turn the boy over to the Russians."

"Colonel, if you do that, the Soviets will give him immediately to the East Germans and that will be curtains for him."

"We have no choice, fella. The final decision will be made in Washington. General Watson will be in touch with the White House in about an hour. You get over to the Berlin command and stick to Watson like glue. Remember, we will release him to the Russians if there is no word to continue the stalemate. We're on our way."

I hightailed it to Berlin command headquarters. It was obvious that General Watson was irritated with the train commander and sympathetic with the passengers who were spending their Thanksgiving Day on the train. My sentiments were the opposite: let the train sit there until doomsday, if necessary, before surrendering the boy. I offered the general my opinion that rather than giving in to East German demands, we take the offensive. I suggested that the Soviet Union was responsible for ensuring that our trains passed through the zone without interruption, and therefore bore the responsibility for making certain no one boarded the trains en route. We didn't give up those thousands of East Germans who were fleeing into West Berlin. Why should we give up someone who was seeking refuge on an American army train?

It was about two hours after my arrival before General Watson entered a cramped small enclosure to talk directly to someone in Washington. I thrust my head into the compartment. I could hear only General Watson's side of the conversation.

"I see. I agree. We'll turn him over."

Upon hearing this my blood pressure must have shot off the scale. I burst in on the general's conversation: "General, recommend it was the Soviets' fault for not protecting our trains! Now he's on our . . ."

It was too late. The general waved me off. "Yes. Right away!"

I never learned who was on the other end of the conversation. It could have been the president. It certainly was someone senior to General Watson. The decision was to have the USMLM chief take the German lad from the train and hand him to the Soviets, not to the Germans.

"You know, General, that the Russians will be the 'middleman' and give the boy to the Germans."

General Watson did not want to discuss the matter further. "The boy will be transferred to the Russians. The train will proceed." Unless the mission chief received a counterorder, his orders were to take the boy from the train and formally hand him to the Soviets that were present at the scene. If the decision was not to give up the German boy, my task was to relay the message to the Soviets in Potsdam so that arrangements could be made to conduct talks with the Russians at a higher level.

I stayed at Berlin mission headquarters until early evening when the chief and Fitzgerald returned.

"You had to give him up, Colonel," I said.

Fitzgerald was silent. The colonel answered, "It was terrible. I will never forget the look in that boy's eyes when we handed him to the Russians. The expression of agony and despair will never leave me. The Germans were there and right in front of us the Russians turned the boy over to them."

Fitzgerald seemed too choked up to say a word and tears were streaming down the colonel's cheeks. "There was nothing you could do, Colonel," I said. "The decision was made at the highest level. I hope that you will convey the hopelessness you observed to General Watson."

I firmly believed that in the minds of the decision makers the inconvenience to the passengers was not the deciding factor to surrender the boy. In fact, the passengers had sided with the train commander to protect the lad. Those making the decision to hand over the boy wanted to end the affair as quickly as possible. It is true that the train would not have been released before possibly prolonged negotiations with the Russians, but anyone who had dealings with the Russians on a daily basis would have expected them to cave in, eventually. The German boy was not worth the aggravation to the Soviets. His life should have been worth our all-out effort to save him.

After the incident I was not sure about the boy's fate. I was told at the time that an article in the East German newspapers stated that he had been executed to prevent others from trying the same stunt. Recently I learned that the boy survived an East German jail sentence and years later had a joyous reunion with the train commander. Regardless of his ultimate fate, Thanksgiving Day, 23 November 1961, was one of the saddest and most anger-filled days of my life.

19

Siegfried

Siegfried, a wiry German in his thirties, was a member of the household staff assigned by the Soviets to USMLM's mission house in East Germany. Along with the other East German servants working there, his workday was not over until after the evening meal, and he was on call for any problems encountered during his off hours. Siegfried was the quintessential jack-of-all-trades. He stoked the fires in the furnace. He repaired appliances. He fixed the plumbing, replaced the fuses, and maintained the grounds. The enlisted men who lived in the house called on Siegfried for every possible task, no matter how challenging or how menial. Siegfried was the most accommodating individual imaginable. He approached all requests with a cheery smile.

It is difficult to fault the mission's enlisted army and air force drivers for any indiscretions. Their courage surpassed anything that I had seen elsewhere in my eighteen years in the U.S. Navy. Living behind the Iron Curtain and performing demanding and dangerous tasks every single day with little or no supervision outside of their driving duties, however, led to a lifestyle of complete independence at the Potsdam mission house. For a week at a time an officer lived in the quarters, usually with his family, and served as the Potsdam duty officer. Mission officers took turns as the duty officer: they checked local Soviet military movements and delivered routine messages to the Russians, but exercised little supervision over the enlisted men. The East German staff prepared and served the meals, made the beds, and cleaned the house. When not traveling on reconnaissance trips the drivers lived a cushy, carefree life, far different from that of any other serviceman of the time. I didn't begrudge their life of ease, but did have reservations about the rapport that developed between them and Siegfried.

My only conflict in over two years with the enlisted mission drivers occurred one morning after a severe thunderstorm passed through the area. I returned to Potsdam from a grueling three-day trip at about 3:00 A.M. I slept soundly until 10:00, when I made my way down to the kitchen for breakfast. Two drivers, also eating in the kitchen's little alcove, began to tell me about the raging thunderstorm that had passed over the area at 6:00 A.M. While they were telling me about the fury of the tempest I happened to look out the window onto the front grounds and was shocked to see the American flag lying on the ground beside the flagpole. The flag flew, lighted at night, twenty-four hours a day at the Potsdam mission house.

"Look, the flag! It's on the ground!" I cried.

"No sweat, Commander. We told Siegfried when he arrived. He will get to it."

"No! You will get to it right now."

"Siegfried takes care of the flag, Commander."

"Raise the flag and then I want to talk to both of you."

The soldiers didn't get to the front grounds in time. Siegfried was on the job and carefully raised the flag close up on the pole. Both soldiers sullenly listened to me, neither understanding why I was upset to learn that Siegfried's duties included handling the American flag. Nor did they understand my distress about the American flag lying on the ground for four hours. Yet both were dedicated drivers who reacted immediately to all demands when we were on the road, even the unreasonable ones. Later I described the incident to some of my army officer colleagues, who assured me that they would instill a different soldierly outlook among the enlisted men. But Siegfried continued to be the head honcho in the Potsdam Mission House.

Lack of supervision and oversight of the enlisted men who lived in the Potsdam House and the East German staff resulted from a poorly conceived USMLM standard operations procedure which placed the responsibility for the Potsdam House's operation under the USMLM operations officer. This officer, who worked in West Berlin, was not accredited to the commander in chief, Soviet Forces, nor did he possess Soviet identification authorization (which made him unauthorized to travel to Potsdam). Eventually the USMLM chief acted on my recommendation of 27 June 1961 to place responsibility for the staff and men directly under the Potsdam duty officer.

If I learned one thing from my training in intelligence while studying at the U.S. Navy Postgraduate School in Washington, D.C., it was to be vigilant regarding counterintelligence personnel. In one exercise at the school the student teams were sent out on surreptitious collection tours. My assignment was to photograph railroad underpasses. No one in the class knew that one team was assigned to be a counterintelligence team and spy on our activities.

I was extremely alert and cautious about being detected when photographing various targets around the Washington area. None of us wanted to explain to the local police what we were doing. We returned to the school after completing the missions, thrilled with our success. We couldn't wait for the accolades we expected to receive. Our hopes were dashed when the counterintelligence team made the first report, exposing all of our activities as a result of listening to our conversations.

Siegfried listened carefully to every discussion in the Potsdam House. On 1 January 1962 a New Year's Eve party was held for all tour officers, Berlin backup staffs, and their spouses. Some of the East German household staff also attended, including a young and attractive buxom blond named Dagmar Petres. Dagmar fit the perfect physical image of the irresistible, alluring female agent one reads about in every fictional spy story. I didn't trust her. I decided to refrain from taking a single drink so that I could maintain surveillance on both Dagmar and Siegfried throughout the evening. It wasn't long before my suspicions gave way. No only was her English proficiency almost nonexistent, but she was fully in the swing of the party, drinking drink for drink and enjoying every minute. This was no put-on. German was her only language. Before the stroke of twelve Dagmar was ill and out of the picture.

Siegfried and I were the only persons present who were completely sober, not having had one drink all evening. Like everything else Siegfried did, his bartending was excellent. He could have passed muster at any swank bar in New York. He listened carefully to the wagging tongues at the bar, taking in every word. Seeing me sitting near the bar area all evening drinking ginger ale surely convinced him that I was some kind of security agent. After midnight and once the party began to wear down fast, Siegfried ask me to join him in one drink to celebrate the beginning of the new year. I declined. He did not follow through and have the drink by himself.

After the party I was more convinced than before that Siegfried was a top Stasi agent. Finally my conviction was confirmed. One of the East German Stasi agents who followed and harassed our reconnaissance tours defected to the West. On that day Siegfried disappeared from our sight forever. If still alive Siegfried would be in his late seventies or early eighties by now. Whether dead or alive, I will always remember Siegfried as a most adept master spy who possessed a special gift that enabled him to be beloved by the easy victims of his intelligence collection.

The army and air force drivers gave a name to their private retreat and living quarters at the Potsdam House: the "Shlagbaum Room." ("Shlagbaum" is the Russian word for a railroad crossing gate.) The entire top floor of the house served two purposes: as the living area for the enlisted men and as a place of refuge for all individuals when the Potsdam House was under attack during demonstrations by angry East Germans. A jail-type iron door was used to block entry to the third floor, the obvious reason for choosing the word "shlagbaum."

Violent demonstrations that included throwing stones, breaking windows, and tearing down the American flag occurred on rare occasions. The only one that happened during my tour of duty at the USMLM was in progress one day when I entered the grounds. On 13 May 1961 the Soviet Union signed an agreement with the Congo. At the time the United States backed President Kasavubu and the Soviet Union backed the country's prime minister, Patrice Lumumba, which resulted in an East-West standoff at the center of the Congo. President Kasavubu removed Lumumba, who subsequently was murdered. After Lumumba's death the communist world staged several violent demonstrations at Western embassies around the globe.

A crowd of East Germans entered the Potsdam mission grounds and began to stone the house. Most of the demonstrators were of school age. As I came up to the rear of the crowd I asked a young boy why he was throwing stones at the building.

"Lumumba was murdered."

"So why are you throwing stones at an American building? Do you hate Americans?"

"No! The teachers let us out of classes to come here."

This answer I understood. During the cold war what red-blooded American boy would not have been overjoyed to get out of school to throw stones at a hated communist target? I didn't doubt that American youngsters would fling their missiles with more enthusiasm than what I was witnessing because during my two years in East Germany, without exception I found German youth to be very friendly and helpful.

The primary use of the top floor of the house was to provide living quarters for the five army and air force enlisted men, and was considered out of bounds to officers, unless invited. I never received an invitation. All I knew about the goings-on in the Shlagbaum Room was hearsay, except for one incident that was related to me by a Soviet officer and later confirmed by one of my more in-tune army officer colleagues.

Two Soviet Army officers from the external relations branch appeared one day in an angry state, complaining to the Potsdam duty officer about a disgraceful display and insult on the top floor of the house. They demanded to view the scene of the scandalous exhibit. The officer dutifully escorted the Russians to the Shlagbaum Room.

Nailed to the wall as a picture frame was a toilet seat sprinkled with glittering spangles and stars. The duty officer lifted the lid of the seat and was shocked to see a photograph of Walter Ulbricht, the head of the German Democratic Republic (who had assumed his position as head of state on 12 September 1960), chairman of the Council of State of the German Democratic Republic, and general secretary of the Communist (Socialist Unity) Party.

Walter Ulbricht was despised throughout East Germany. One of his memorable responses about the forthcoming Berlin crisis was made on 15 June 1961 at an international press conference. Prior to the erection of the Berlin Wall a sign, containing a direct quote from Ulbricht's press conference, appeared facing the inside of East Berlin. As translated from the German, it said: "I understand your question precisely. There are people in West Germany that expect us to mobilize the construction worker of the capital of the German Democratic Republic to build a wall. Not that I am aware of the existence of such an intention. The construction workers of our capital are mainly busy with house construction and their manpower is fully used for that. NOBODY INTENDS TO ERECT A WALL!"

Regardless of the intended humor, displaying a toilet seat with a photograph of the head of the East German state certainly was not a bright idea. The mischief resulted from the sacrosanct status of the enlisted drivers' Shlagbaum Room. It demonstrated the lack of army supervision over the enlisted occupants of the Potsdam house. The report of this indiscretion to the Russians also indicated the fact that one of the East German workers in the Potsdam House had access to the Shlagbaum Room. Of course, the likely candidate was Siegfried.

Had the photo on the wall been of Lenin, Stalin, or Khrushchev there would have been hell to pay. But Walter Ulbricht was a joke among East Germans outside the party organization. The Soviets paid little attention to his government. The Russian military ran helter-skelter over East Germany, polluting the countryside, tearing up the roads with tanks, and interfering with transportation schedules. Many two-tracked railroad lines were now single tracked because after World War II the Russians removed and shipped one line of tracks to the Soviet Union.

The Shlagbaum Room incident did not turn into an international disagreement because the Russians and Germans were satisfied with the immediate removal of the toilet seat frame with its photo of Ulbricht. Members of the USMLM were able to keep the episode within the family. The value of the collection effort and the unquestioned beyond-the-call-of-duty service of the drivers on the road superseded any inclination to observe normal military disciplinary practices in the Potsdam House.

Life in the Shlagbaum Room continued unchanged, absent the image of the head of East Germany staring out from behind the lid of a toilet seat.

20

Shootings, the Last Straw

Every mission officer knew of the best place off the autobahn to hide from tails: a dirt road concealed by the overhanging branches of some huge trees. As soon as a reconnaissance team was able to speed ahead out of sight on the autobahn beltway out around Berlin, it was possible to duck directly from the super expressway into "Shady Lane," as everyone called the hiding place.

Two new and inexperienced U.S. Air Force intelligence officers departed on a reconnaissance tour driven by the many-times-decorated driver Mel Ratz. The senior of the two air force officers with Ratz was fifty years old and spoke neither Russian nor German (he was an Arabic linguist). Ratz had shown feats of bravery in earlier trips under the guidance and reins of the senior air force mission officer, Maj. Matt Warren. Warren had been transferred and circumstances had changed. Mel was guiding brand-new air force mission officers on a reconnaissance trip—and he was ready to roll without Matt Warren's supervision.

The chase to lose East German surveillance began as soon as the new air force team entered the autobahn. Aware of "Shady Lane" as the ideal hiding spot, Mel sped at maximum speed to the turn for the secluded hideaway in order to show the two neophytes how easily he could lose tails. Unfortunately, for the first time in USMLM history the Stasi agents saw the car turn off the autobahn onto the dirt road.

Accepted procedure at Shady Lane was to wait in the concealed shelter for at least thirty minutes and then drive ahead to an asphalt road at the lane's other end. Mel stayed for the usual period before proceeding the half-mile to the exit. When the reconnaissance team arrived at the end of the lane they found it being blocked by East German police who were aiming their machine guns directly at the approaching vehicle. Mel Ratz didn't pause for an instant. He stepped on the gas pedal and drove the mission vehicle straight at the human blockade. Before diving for safety the East Germans opened fire and shattered the mission vehicle's front windshield. Ratz drove through the barrage onto the asphalt road ahead. The Germans did not recover in time to fire into the rear of the speeding car. Miraculously, none of the vehicle's occupants were struck by incoming bullets. Mel drove the bullet-ridden vehicle through Potsdam to the Soviet checkpoint between East Germany and West Berlin. The Soviet border guards barely raised an eyebrow at seeing the damage. In Berlin the usual protest was made by the mission chief, but everything continued as before. It was just another shooting incident, the kind that should be expected at times behind the Iron Curtain.

Of course Shady Lane's days as a favorite hiding place were over. Those two air force officers never again crossed into the Soviet Zone and declined to continue their tour of duty at the USMLM. Sgt. Mel Ratz continued his aggressive devil-may-care driving style with other new air force officers, men with whom I later shared an unusual stint of detention.

I never understood why such a ruckus and protest was made about my earlier shooting incident near Witzin when so little attention was being paid to this one. In my case there was only shooting over the top of the car. Here the police fired directly at the vehicle, pouring machine gun rounds into its front.

Shooting incidents were isolated but not rare during my tour of duty. The most serious one occurred near the end of my assignment to the USMLM. The tails who had been off the road after my incident in February 1961 returned with a vengeance in the spring of 1962. When they saw me on the road, they sought others. All the other reconnaissance tours had become "fair game." Of course, we all knew and understood that "licensed spies" carry out their assignments at their own risk.

One other serious shooting incident occurred before I left. The East Germans had riddled Capt. Bill Schneider's mission car. Again, no one was injured, but no one doubted that the shots were meant to kill. This time the West initiated immediate action. The commander in chief, U.S. Army–Europe ordered U.S. troops to surround the Soviet Military Liaison Mission in Frankfurt, West Germany, permitting no one to enter or leave the mission grounds. The USMLM chief and Lieutenant Colonel Fitzgerald traveled to the office of the commander in chief, Group of Soviet Forces–Germany to meet and discuss the incident with General Voronsov of Soviet headquarters in Zossen-Wunsdorf, East Germany.

After my altercation with the chief over the shooting incident and report in February 1961 my relations with him had been friendly. Usually he kept me abreast of all USMLM matters because when he and Fitzgerald were out of the Potsdam area, I was the senior USMLM officer in Berlin and Potsdam. Before they left that day the chief dropped by my Berlin office. I told the colonel that I expected further retaliation by the Soviets over the Schneider incident. "Colonel, the Soviets are bound to surround our mission grounds in Potsdam at any moment."

"Not while I have an appointment with General Voronsov. Voronsov was particularly agreeable to our protest when they fired at you."

"But, Colonel, our troops have surrounded the Soviet mission in West Germany. The Soviets have a 'tit for tat' mind-set."

"I'm confident nothing will happen until we return."

The colonel was right. Nothing happened. Our operation continued as usual. That afternoon the chief and Fitz returned. The chief was delighted with the discussion he had had with General Voronsov.

"I've talked to General Voronsov many times during the past year. General Voronsov is very nice. He understands our concern about the continuing shooting incidents. I explained that it's always the Germans who fire and not the Soviet military. He has asked me to return tomorrow for the final decision on the matter. Would you like to replace Fitzgerald and go with me tomorrow as my interpreter?"

"Great! What did he say about the surrounding of the Soviet mission in Frankfurt?"

"Nothing. We just talked about the seriousness of the Schneider shooting."

I was delighted to go with the chief. Although I had had previous contact with Marshal Konev and General Yakubovsky (both senior to Voronsov), I was anxious to size up Voronsov. The colonel had always praised him as the nicest of the three top Soviets in East Germany. The next morning when we arrived at Soviet headquarters we were ushered into a huge office. Our driver waited, parked in front of the entrance. Two armed Soviet junior officers directed us to the desk of General Voronsov. There were no chairs in the vicinity.

The chief spoke and I interpreted: "General, it's a pleasure to return today and also a pleasure to present Commander Fahey. I know that you are familiar with him by reputation."

The general glared and shouted, "Molchitye!," the Russian equivalent of "Shut up!" Then he continued, "You both are under arrest." Turning to the two armed officers he said, "Take them at gun point to their vehicle and give them and their driver the instruction given to you earlier." We were summarily marched out of the building to the waiting car. A Soviet soldier held a machine gun, pressed to our driver's head. The driver informed us that as soon as we had disappeared into the building he was placed under armed guard.

A Soviet captain turned to me and said, "Tell this fellow with you and your driver to follow the Soviet vehicle in front of you until you reach the destination. Do not deviate. The orders to those who will escort you are to kill you if you make the slightest deviation from behind the car in front of you. Understand? You are all under arrest!"

We entered our mission car. The soldier with the machine gun moved from his station beside our driver to a military vehicle behind us. Without delay all three vehicles departed from Soviet headquarters. In the vehicle that was sometimes behind and sometimes abreast of us, Soviet soldiers kept AK-47 machine guns trained on us. If we fell back the slightest amount from the car in front of us, the vehicle behind us would accelerate to our left side. The miniature convoy proceeded at an extremely slow pace when passing through every German town on the way north to Potsdam. The greatest humiliation I felt was the obvious demonstration to Germans in the towns who were observing this scene that we, Americans, were Soviet captives. We were silent. I don't know which of the three of us was angriest.

Finally, after driving ninety minutes to cover what is normally a thirty-minute trip, we arrived at the Potsdam Mission House grounds. It was surrounded by shoulder-to-shoulder Soviet troops, all carrying AK-47 guns. The Soviet escort vehicles stopped at the gate and we passed through. As we left the car I resisted the temptation to say to the colonel, "General Voronsov is very nice."

The chief entered the Potsdam House and immediately telephoned Lieutenant Colonel Fitzgerald in Berlin. They had worked out a special code for situations in which ultrasecrecy was required. In addition to a standard German telephone, the Potsdam House had a radio telephone with the capability to garble conversation en route, but the chief didn't trust its reliability.

The system of secret communications between the two seemed to be completely secure. Each had access to the same books. One novel was in the colonel's office in West Berlin and the colonel had stashed the other copy of the novel somewhere in the Potsdam House. When needed in an emergency, the plan was to communicate on the telephone by finding each word to be used in the message in the novel. The sender would find a word on a page and then give the listener the page number, the line, and the location in the line.

The chief wanted to tell Lieutenant Colonel Fitzgerald to find a way to get the Soviets to permit him to leave the troop-surrounded Potsdam House. The colonel wanted to return to Berlin where he could provide the U.S. commander in chief with a firsthand report and then be involved in future negotiations with the Soviets to resolve the matter.

The chief asked me to sit beside him and find the word he needed, and he would relay the page number and other coded comments to Fitzgerald on the telephone. Finding the first few words of his message took at least fifteen minutes, which exhausted the patience of the colonel. He took over the book and sought the appropriate words himself, but he didn't have any more success than I. After an hour the colonel finally gave up and in plain English told Fitz what he wanted him to do.

I was happy to get away from the phone. I went upstairs to get a better look at the Soviet troops, positioned around the grounds. Their location surprised me. A line of soldiers crossed the mission grounds. Obviously the Soviet unit had not been briefed or shown the perimeters of the U.S. territory. The Potsdam House plot included some ramshackle buildings along the south side of the road leading to the guard gate. The Soviet line of troops cut directly south across from the gate to the water's edge. I was sure that the posting of the soldiers was unintentional, but I hurried downstairs to tell the colonel.

"Colonel, the Soviet soldiers are lined up inside one-third of our territory. I'll go out and move them back."

The chief didn't think that this was a major point. He was concerned more about getting back to Berlin.

"No, John, we stay inside the house."

After an hour of waiting, Fitzgerald called to report that the Russians had agreed to let everyone leave the Potsdam House and return to Berlin. Only the colonel, the colonel's driver, the duty officer, and I were inside the besieged house at the time. Fitz added that none of the other USMLM officers were presently in the Soviet Zone.

The chief turned to me and said, "The driver will take me and the duty officer to Berlin. You stay, John. I am afraid that the Soviets will shut down the USMLM if we have no one in the zone. They might claim that we abandoned the operation."

"Fine. Any instructions?"

"No. If anything else unusual occurs, telephone. We'll get this settled in short order. I'll call Barbara and tell her you will be delayed for a while."

The three drove out the gate with no interference. Alone in the house and in charge, my first thought was to move the Soviets off the mission grounds. But I wasn't alone. There was one more creature left in the house with me—Toby, the German shepherd dog who lived in the house. He was the friendliest dog I had ever encountered. He leapt on every stranger to lick any portion of skin visible to his romantic eyes.

I found Toby's leash and we both stepped out the front door to face the Soviet contingent. A Soviet major stood in the center of the long line. As we walked toward him, Toby began to strain the leash forward, toward the soldiers. When we were within ten feet, full of excitement Toby tugged to jump on the nearest Russian soldiers and lick their very young and rosy cheeks. Three soldiers dropped their guns and moved back. The major held his ground. I stopped, saving the Soviet major from being slobbered to death by Toby.

"I'm sorry, Major. The dog is very friendly. He won't bite. Please tell your soldiers."

The major didn't have to give an order. The soldiers understood me, retrieved their weapons, and returned to the line.

The major asked, "What do you want?"

"Major, I know that you haven't placed your men on our United States territory on purpose, but you must get off our land. The border of our American grounds on the south side is behind you, way down the road from here. Your placement of the troops directly south from the gate to the lake cuts across United States territory."

"I was ordered to surround your headquarters. I know nothing about your territory."

"Major, you are violating international territorial rights. I have warned you to get off our land! You personally will suffer for this infringement if you do not withdraw to the proper boundary."

"I'll have to contact my seniors."

The major placed a sergeant in command and left. I returned to the house, pulling the extremely disappointed Toby with me. In thirty minutes the entire line moved at least four hundred feet down the road from the gate. I telephoned the chief in West Berlin and informed him of the Soviet withdrawal to a new position.

The colonel replied, "Good. Tomorrow morning I am sending the duty officer to relieve you. General Bruce Clark is arriving in Berlin tomorrow. He asked me to have you join his staff members in preparing a paper that he will present to Marshal Konev. A meeting of the commanders in chief will be held in the Potsdam House two days from now."

I went to bed early to get a good night's sleep. I didn't need an alarm system to detect intruders since I had about a hundred

Soviet soldiers on guard to keep any unauthorized persons from entering the Potsdam House. My faithful companion Toby (who was more like a scaredy cat than a dog) slept at the foot of the bed. At least the two of us showed the Soviet Army that we meant business when we told the Soviets to "Get off our land!"

Arriving back in West Berlin, I was immediately directed to the headquarters of the Berlin command. Gen. Bruce Clark and some of his staff members were already in the briefing room, which had been reserved for our deliberations. General Clark laid down the general theme of the message that he planned to present to Marshal Konev in Potsdam. It left no doubt that the United States would not stand for any more firing of weapons at USMLM personnel.

Before leaving the room Clark said, "Have my speech finished by 1130 hours." Clark's staff members were industrious and exceptionally bright. Any input that I offered was considered carefully. By 11:15 A.M. we had all agreed on a hard-hitting speech for Clark that placed the onus entirely on the Soviets and emphasized that measures needed to be taken to ensure there would be no reoccurrence of these shooting incidents.

General Clark returned promptly at 1130 hours. Reading the presentation he squirmed and finally spoke. "I don't like it. You are supposed to be the 'smart boys.' Get it together. I don't want any threats that we cannot keep. It doesn't relate strongly enough the seriousness of the shooting and consequences." Clark left without saying when he would return. I had never heard the term "smart boy" in the navy, but got the message. We reworked the speech most of the afternoon.

By the time General Clark returned I was mentally exhausted. Clark looked at the final product and said, "It will do." Before leaving he thanked me for joining his staff in the effort. That evening the chief, Fitzgerald, and I met informally with several people: West Berlin mayor Willy Brandt, some unidentified government people, the commander of the Berlin command, commander in chief, U.S. Army–Europe Gen. Bruce Clark, and Clark's deputy. A meeting with Marshal Konev was scheduled for the next morning at the Potsdam House. The arrangement was to be five delegates on each side of the table, with Clark, his deputy, the USMLM chief, Fitzgerald, and me representing the West. Ordinarily Fitzgerald and I would have been interpreters, but the Russians insisted that each of the five participants on both sides would be a delegate with the authority to speak on his own. In addition, Fitzgerald and I were to interpret what the Soviet delegates said in Russian to Clark, and two English-speaking Soviets would interpret what Clark, his deputy, and the USMLM chief said to Konev. Fitzgerald and I could directly speak our views to Konev in Russian.

A table was prepared with Soviet and American flags in the center of the Potsdam House ballroom. A single table held five chairs opposite five other chairs. No one sat at the head of the table. When I entered the room I was surprised to see a crowd of civilian onlookers filling seats that surrounded the meeting table.

As soon as everyone was seated Konev said, "I want the room cleared. I want no one in the room but the five official delegates on each side."

Konev's pronouncement surprised everyone. Slowly everybody except the ten delegates filed out of the room. Then Konev said, "General Clark, you called this meeting. Please go first."

Clark looked to his deputy for his speech. His deputy shook his head and whispered, "I do not have it." Clark then looked at our colonel, who made a similar negative head shake.

Konev took the initiative at this point and said, "If you are not prepared to begin, I am. I have a serious matter to bring to your attention. You are planning a military parade in West Berlin and plan to display, in this parade, missiles. If you do this, you will suffer severe consequences. I want your assurances now at this moment that you will not carry out this intention."

Not knowing anything about detailed plans for the parade, we all looked at General Clark. He replied, "I cannot give you an answer now, but will respond to your request before the parade."

Konev added, "I cannot stress how dangerous to you and offensive to us this affront is. Perilous ramifications will befall West Berlin if your missiles are displayed in this military parade."

Clark turned the discussion to the Germans' firing on Western military liaison mission personnel: "These incidents have continued throughout the past year-and-a-half. German special police fired at Commander Fahey. Police fired at USMLM's air force team. German border police fired at the British military liaison personnel, seriously wounding Corporal Douglas Day. Now all movement in both zones has been curtailed as a result of this latest shooting incident."

During the night of 10 March 1962, as British corporal Day was driving the British duty officer in the Potsdam area close to the West Berlin border, without warning the Grenzschutzpolizei (grepo) fired machine guns at the car, severely injuring Day. The tires were blown and the gas tank riddled full of holes. Corporal Day eventually recovered, but suffered five perforations to his intestines, a wounded right thigh, a bullet in his liver, fractures to his left and right big toes, and eventually the removal of one kidney.

Before a short recess Konev tried to confine the dispute to the encirclement of his mission in Frankfurt, West Germany. During the break the American discussion centered around what Konev was threatening in his remarks about future severe consequences for West Berlin. "Are they threatening World War III?" I took the position that Konev was trying to save face and counter with an offensive of his own. Our concern about the shootings in his zone had placed him entirely in a defensive position from which he was trying to change direction. I added that I thought, as I usually did in such circumstances, that it was a Russian bluff. For almost two years I was impressed by the outspoken Soviet military's fear of a global confrontation.

General Clark wanted to end the meeting on a positive note, but he also did not want to fail to get assurances from Konev to stop the Germans from taking violent actions against our mission personnel. I expressed my opinion that Konev could not guarantee the security of our people in the Soviet Zone as long as our aggressive intelligence collection effort there continued. Some incidents had involved confrontations with armed Soviet soldiers as well as Germans. My final input was to tell Konev that we would trust him to stop indiscriminate shooting episodes, but only the future could justify our faith in his success.

Clark listened to everyone. He liked my suggestions, which pleased the mission chief. General Clark was diplomatic but firm in his final remarks. Before the meeting adjourned there was mutual agreement to remove the encirclements from each mission headquarters. No further mention was made of the missiles in the American military parade in West Berlin. Because General Clark was so pleased with the outcome of the meeting with Konev he did not pursue the matter of who bore the responsibility for the disappearance of his speech.

I was a spectator at the American military parade in West Berlin. No missiles appeared in the parade. About a week later, on 1 May 1962, the East Germans held a large May Day celebration and military parade in East Berlin. Missiles were the highlight of the parade.

21

THE "CHICKEN" SPY

The second request I received from the navy during my entire time at the USMLM surprised me and I wasn't prepared to fulfill it: take a motion picture of a Soviet anti-aircraft antenna (to verify the nodding timing being used). For almost two years I had been taking only still photos and had to search Berlin for a high-quality 16 mm camera.

Air force major Matt Warren had been replaced by Lt. Col. Ben Gordon, a pleasant, friendly, cooperative officer. Since the USMLM air force team frequently passed into areas where radar installations were prevalent, I decided to ask Ben if I could ride with him on one of his Soviet airfield intelligence collection tours. I told Ben that I wanted to be a passenger in the back seat and otherwise not be involved in any way with the team's assignment.

As we left West Berlin I felt less pressure than I had felt on any other trip I had taken behind the Iron Curtain. Ben was senior to me and entirely responsible for anything that might happen in the Soviet Zone. I reveled in the thought that I didn't have to plan the tour, direct the driver, or make any decisions. All I had to do was sit and take motion pictures of any Soviet antennae we could see from the side of the road. None of the air force team members on the trip spoke Russian so I could help by reading any signs we encountered en route. Otherwise I planned to keep quiet.

As we approached a Soviet military base the driver, Mel Ratz, drove off the paved road onto an open field that led into a thick forest. I couldn't contain myself. "Where are we going?"

Mel answered, "Through the trees ahead."

"There's no road. There's no opening."

"We'll make one." Sure enough, the car could maneuver among the upright trees, but felled trees around the area's perimeter blocked our entry.

Ben said, "Everyone out of the vehicle. We'll lift those trees out of the way." This was not my way of penetrating a Soviet military area. I always toured very cautiously, never entering an area without having an exit in mind, and always heading the vehicle in the direction of the exit when on foot inside the area. It looked like I was a "chicken," and I was. I voiced my concern about the plan, but the others forced me to help them remove the trees. We jumped back into the vehicle and Mel drove through the forest. Finally we entered a hard surface road. Soon we passed a platoon of Soviet soldiers.

I spoke up, "Ben, I think we are inside the base."

Ben responded, "Mel, let's get out of here."

Mel pushed down on the accelerator. Suddenly we were about thirty feet from a radar antenna on the side of the road, with another one visible ahead of us.

I cried, "Slow down, Mel. I can't get my pictures."

Mel was following Ben's instruction and there was no way I was going to get pictures out the side window. About a mile down the road we encountered a main gate with a sentry posted. We drove lickety-split right through the open gate. Everyone but me laughed. It was bad enough that we had bashed through the woods and entered a military installation, but once inside I had gotten nothing.

Our next trauma occurred six miles from the base, where a Soviet sentry was blocking the road. When Mel stopped the sentry came to the driver's window and aimed an AK-47 at Mel's head. Another Soviet went to a radio. I said, "Ben, we're in real trouble now. They have blocked all the roads from the base. I can't argue our way out of this one. Don't utter a word about anyone knowing Russian."

Within fifteen minutes a Soviet officer arrived. He blabbered at Ben, "You violated a military installation! This is a criminal act!"

Ben smiled and shrugged his shoulders, indicating that he didn't understand. Mel was silent. I sat dejectedly in the back seat, expecting to suffer the worse detention of my life during the waning days of my tour of duty. To my absolute amazement the Soviet officer, without another word, waved us on our way. I had been detained for hours in solitary confinement just for being caught near a military base. The air force team moved on, laughing at the inconvenience of getting less than half an hour detention on the road. No more opportunities for motion pictures arose during the trip.

I got the motion pictures on my own, slowly traveling the dirt roads for hours on end but always keeping exits from sensitive areas readily available. The fondest memory of that air force tour was speeding out the main gate of a Soviet military installation and finding out that there is some merit in being a "chicken" spy.

22

The Berlin Military Police

One of my passionate desires near the end of my tour of duty in the beleaguered city was to get out without enduring a second confrontation with the Berlin military police and the Berlin Brigade provost marshal.

As a member of the U.S. Navy I was not accustomed to dealing with a permanent professional police force. I served as senior shore patrol officer during port visits in Spain, in Italy, and even in Havana, Cuba, where junior officers, petty officers, yeomen, boatswains, radiomen, everyone served as the navy's police force ashore. All of us strived to ensure discipline in foreign ports while exercising good common sense. Since shore patrol duty was a temporary assignment, we did not assume the aura of a professional police force. The army's military police, under the command of the office of the provost marshal in Berlin, functioned as police in every sense of the word. They could cite you for good driving (as one MP had done after following my spouse) or they could conduct a criminal investigation if you violated any one of the hundreds of U.S. Army circulars issued by the commander in chief, U.S. Army–Europe or directives issued by lesser commands.

My first run-in with a Berlin MP occurred as I was returning from a reconnaissance trip, having spent the previous forty-eight hours sleepless in the woods of East Germany. After the trip I drove back to Berlin from the Potsdam House in a USMLM car. The car was covered with mud, but the front license plate was visible. I crossed into West Berlin dead tired, driving about 20 mph and dreading the thought of a reception my wife and I were expected to attend that was being hosted by the British on Saturday evening. I hadn't traveled a mile before a military police car flashed a light behind me. I was dressed in a U.S. Army uniform that bore a lieutenant colonel insignia.

The MP approached the car with a pad in hand, writing as he inspected the outside of the vehicle. I rolled down the driver's window.

"Your name?"

"John Fahey. What's wrong with the car?" He continued to write and didn't answer. "What is wrong with the car? Why have you stopped me?"

Continuing to write and not looking up, he replied, "Nothing is wrong with the vehicle."

"Is there some kind of violation?"

Still not looking up and continuing to write, he answered, "Yes."

I was too exhausted to continue the questions and decided to sit quietly. Ten minutes passed without a word. The MP continued to write. Finally he spoke to me. "You are charged with driving a military staff car while smoking!"

"There's an army rule about smoking while driving a car?"

"You heard me!"

"I'm pretty tired. Can I go now?"

His hesitation in replying to my question worried me. He might be thinking of giving me a second citation for "driving a staff car when tired."

A British Military Liaison Mission car, returning also from East Germany, pulled alongside us. The British officer asked, "Do you need any help, chap?" The MP motioned him to move on. When released I headed home to bed. I slept soundly until it was time to dress for the reception. At the reception British brigadier Tom Pearson asked me why I was stopped earlier in the day by an MP in the American sector.

I replied, "Driving while smoking."

Brigadier Pearson could hardly contain himself. Beckoning to the USMLM chief, he said, "Come here. John was arrested for smoking. We avoid detention for spying successfully behind the curtain and get caught for smoking in West Berlin. This is the last straw, isn't it?"

Tom Pearson ribbed the chief further about needing to protect American officers from harassment while they were traveling in West Berlin, not when they were in East Germany. When our colonel was able to free himself from the brigadier, he informed me, "Tomorrow I will call the Berlin Brigade provost marshal, Lieutenant Colonel Robert Sabolyk, about this."

Early Monday morning I was summoned to appear before the provost marshal, Lieutenant Colonel Sabolyk. I put on my navy dress blues that bore the USMLM patch. He greeted me coldly when I entered his office.

Then he said, "I don't appreciate being called on a Sunday about your infraction."

I replied, "I'm sorry that you were disturbed. I certainly didn't call you."

"Well, you were the cause of the call. Why were you driving a staff car? Do naval officers always drive themselves? Don't you have drivers?"

"I was driving back to Berlin from Potsdam. USMLM officers often drive these specially equipped cars in East Germany and also to and from Berlin. By the way, I was wearing an army uniform with a lieutenant colonel insignia."

"Do you have any complaint about the military policeman who stopped you?"

"I don't have a complaint, but he acted more like a policeman than a soldier."

"Why do you say that?"

"Because even the Soviet sentries at the border salute us when we cross into East Germany."

That remark was enough for Lieutenant Colonel Sabolyk. I was dismissed summarily. Except for some kidding I received from others in the mission community, I never heard another word about my "smoking while driving."

I had hoped not to have any more contact with the Berlin Brigade provost marshal, but on 13 May 1962 his office telephoned me about an ongoing criminal investigation of a violation of U.S. Army Europe Circular 550-180 by Chief Petty Officer John T. Weiller, U.S. Navy. I responded, "You should call the U.S. Navy Europe representative in Berlin, not me."

"We can't locate him. You'll get a copy of memorandum AEBAR-PM-A to the commanding general, Berlin Brigade from Robert Sabolyk, provost marshal, and a statement by Weiller, John T., serial number 401 44 59, a male Caucasian, born 17 July 1921, stationed at U.S. Naval Air Station, Los Alamitos, Long Beach, California, taken on 12 May 1962 by Criminal Investigator Alfred P. Pforte."

"My duty assignment is in the Soviet Zone. Please contact the Berlin navy representative."

"Colonel Sabolyk told me to send it to you."

Lieutenant Colonel Sabolyk's memorandum to the commanding general, along with Weiller's statement taken by Criminal Investigator Pforte, arrived on 14 May. Provost Marshal Sabolyk charged Weiller with violating Circular 550-180 by wrongfully entering the Soviet Zone of Germany when he paid 10 West German marks (worth about two dollars and fifty cents at the current exchange rate) for an East German visa stamp of his passport to travel through the Soviet Zone to West Berlin.

The facts of the case were as follows: Chief Petty Officer Weiller had been granted sixty days leave and permission to visit West Berlin by the Department of the Navy. He rode on the proper Helmstedt-to-Berlin autobahn through East Germany to West Berlin with a Dutch friend in a 1962 Fiat vehicle licensed by the Netherlands. Arriving at the confusing multiple checkpoints at the west border of Berlin, naturally the Dutch-licensed car and driver were directed away from the American military checkpoint toward the East German checkpoint. When their vehicle arrived at the Berlin border, the East Germans cleared the car through to the West Berlin checkpoint. Weiller, his friend, and the car were cleared to continue into West Berlin, but upon seeing the U.S. flags at the American military checkpoint, Weiller asked his friend to stop. At the checkpoint he was set upon by American MPs, who accused him of not processing through the American checkpoint at the other end and also of obtaining an East German visa.

For this innocent mistake he had been turned over to Criminal Investigator Pforte. The interrogation revealed that U.S. Army Europe Circular 550-180 had not been given to or even explained to Weiller. His instructions did prohibit Weiller from obtaining a visa from the German Democratic Republic. Weiller understood this to mean he needed to get a visa for travel in East Germany or East Berlin, not for proceeding on the open-access autobahn that headed to West Berlin. Weiller had a letter from the navy's Bureau of Personnel directing him to not apply for a visa from the "so-called German Democratic Republic." Weiller didn't recognize the East German stamping of his passport at Helmstedt as the equivalent of an application for a visa.

Depending on the country, obtaining a visa can be a very tricky business. Many friendly countries at the time of Weiller's innocent mistake did not require visas for American travelers. Other countries stamped visas on American passports. The Soviet Union required visa applications, followed by long delays before issuing visa documents displaying a photograph of the holder.

In my opinion far worse violations frequently occurred when U.S. Army personnel drove off a designated autobahn route and wandered around in East Germany. Often USMLM teams had to deviate from scheduled intelligence trips to search for these nomads roaming aimlessly in the Soviet Zone of Germany. Weiller was being transported by his Dutch friend directly to Berlin on the appropriate and designated route.

Although there certainly was no criminal intent on Weiller's part, the violation was treated by the Berlin provost marshal as a lawless act. The Berlin military police followed the letter of the law and were not about to excuse Weiller's error. Had he not stopped at the American checkpoint he would have entered into Berlin scot-free, with no one the wiser. But the MPs had caught him when he voluntarily appeared at the American military checkpoint, and up the chain of command to the very top they were not going to let him get away.

Berlin provost marshal Sabolyk distributed his memorandum and the statement obtained from officer Weiller to six individuals, including two commanding generals. In his memorandum Sabolyk sought support for further follow-up action through standard navy channels to Weiller's commanding officer in California. However, as someone who had observed several other serious infractions—such as when a new secret sniper scope was mistakenly placed directly into Soviet hands by the U.S. Army, or when all the schedules of the U.S. Atlantic Fleet ship movements were compromised by being handed over directly to the Soviet military by a naval officer who received no retribution—I was not inclined to support the destruction of a navy enlisted man's career for having paid $2.50 for a stamp on his passport.

For two years I violated all sorts of laws on the communist side. In no way were the violations innocent mistakes. But, unlike Weiller, I had a "license to spy." To the Berlin military police's credit, had the American MPs been active in East Germany I am sure that my intelligence collection abilities would have suffered greatly. It was a tenacious outfit! In contrast, the Soviet security personnel were pussycats.

U.S. recognition of the legality of the German Democratic Republic, as the Soviet Zone of East Germany liked to call itself, was not going to hinge on the ten-mark stamp on officer Weiller's passport. Neither the commanding generals nor the provost marshal followed up on my refusal to pursue punitive action on the Weiller criminal charge.

23

Ball of Fire

It was my last reconnaissance tour behind the Iron Curtain, an orientation trip through the northern section of East Germany to familiarize my replacement with the routine. It was supposed to be the easiest and safest trip I had taken since my first orientation venture two years earlier. A week before I had shown my secret observation vantage points near Soviet Army training areas to my relief, Marine Corps major John Clayborne. Now we wore our dress uniforms to visit the cities on the northern coast of East Germany. It was a German holiday on a cold May day in 1962 when we left Rostock to drive east to Stralsund, where I planned to stay the night in the Baltic Hotel. I told our driver, Sgt. Luther Warner, to get gas at the shipyard in Rostock.

"No way, Commander, we'll be detained. No one drives into an East German shipyard, factory, or other city installation."

"Luther, we're members of the Soviet Army. Let's go! And if we are arrested, so what? Major Clayborne should see how we handle a detention."

Arriving at the pumps, we were not challenged. We fueled the car and headed east on Route 105, one of the best open highways in the country. I was seated beside Luther. John Clayborne was in the back seat.

When we neared within fifteen miles of Rostock, Major Clayborne hollered, "We're on fire!"

I looked back to see the flames already licking the rear windows. Before Luther could bring the car to a stop the entire vehicle was a raging ball of fire. We only had time to throw ourselves from the car. Saving our baggage, caps, and uniforms was the least of my worries. Three Leica cameras, two telephoto lenses, and a large case of detailed maps of the Soviet Zone were left in the car. The three of us stood on the highway in shirtsleeves as a cold north wind blew off the Baltic Sea. We were vulnerable and sure to be compromised by the contents of the burning vehicle.

To the south a railroad track was close to the road. I feared that a passing train would be blown to smithereens if the conflagration exploded. Sure enough, a train passed at the height of the blaze. I suffered through a sinking feeling as the train's passenger cars slowly rolled by the inferno. Apparently the fumes were minimized because we had a full tank of gasoline, but the mission car continued to burn wildly. Route 105 was a major two-lane wide highway, but the blaze extended across the opposite westbound lane. I was startled when a Soviet truck loaded with soldiers and heading west burst through the huge fireball.

The truck stopped and I questioned the driver: "Why would you ever drive through this dangerous ball of fire?"

I received the usual Russian answer: "sluzhba (duty)."

The fire still raged, but the flames across the westbound lane lessened. I talked the first German civilian who crossed our path (headed for Rostock) into taking Luther with him. I instructed Luther to go to the Niederlandisch Hotel and call the USMLM for help.

After twenty minutes an East German fire brigade arrived at the scene. The firemen swiftly ran to the burning vehicle with hoses. The ferocity of the fire was still seething, but once the firemen doused it with water I was sure that the compromising cameras, lenses, and maps would survive. The luck of the Irish was with me. No matter what the firemen tried they could not get pressure to the hoses. The mission car continued burning for another forty-five minutes. Finally, when smoke was the only thing still being emitted from the metal shell, one fireman started to reach into the remains to retrieve something that he saw inside. I hollered, "Raus!" and he withdrew.

Then the Germans began to argue that the car was a menace to traffic and had to be removed. I cautioned them that only a Russian could make such a decision. They refused to leave the scene. A short time later two Soviet military trucks arrived. Two officers, a lieutenant colonel and a captain, greeted us. The lieutenant colonel was young, probably in his thirties, while the more junior captain appeared to be in his late fifties. The senior Soviet officer was very friendly and asked me whether he could do anything for me.

"I would die for a cigarette."

"Sorry, but neither of us smoke. It's bad for your health."

"I am going to quit, eventually."

"There is a German store five kilometers down the road. Comrade Captain, get him some cigarettes!"

The captain took off in one of the trucks. The Germans were still lolling around the smoldering mission car. Major Clayborne wandered around the scene. The Soviet lieutenant colonel asked me to join him in the cab of the lone remaining Soviet truck.

"Thank you. I cannot. I am responsible for the car and its contents. I've got to keep the Germans away from it."

The Soviet officer continued to urge me to sit with him: "With this north wind it's freezing out here. Come on inside."

"Thanks again. No."

In a few minutes the Soviet captain returned from the German store. "Comrade Podpolkovnik, I could not get the cigarettes. It's a German holiday. The store was closed."

"What were your orders?"

"Go to the German store and get cigarettes."

"Then go to the store and get cigarettes."

The captain replied, "Yest!" which is similar to "aye, aye, sir" in the U.S. Navy.

Off the captain went, presumably to break open the door to the German store for the cigarettes. In any case he returned promptly with two packs of German cigarettes.

As I lit up a cigarette the lieutenant colonel asked for my name. This was strange because, contrary to every other encounter with the Soviet military, the first demand was for identification.

"My name is Ivan Ivanovich."

"Well, Ivan Ivanovich, we are going to have to remove your car from the road. It's a hazard and also it is tying up traffic."

"I cannot permit its removal. Only our mission chief can do that."

"Your mission chief is not here. You are obligated to give permission."

"I'm sure that he is on his way."

"How is this possible?"

"Before you arrived I sent our driver to Rostock to telephone him."

"How was that possible?"

"A German civilian gave him a ride to Rostock."

"Okay. We'll wait for him, but it's too cold for me, and you are in shirtsleeves. Let's get into the truck."

"Again, thanks. No."

"If I turn the truck around and park it directly behind your car, will you sit with me? You can then look down over your vehicle."

"Is there room also for Major Clayborne?"

"Yes, plenty of room."

"Okay."

The thoughtfulness and kindness of the Russian officer was completely out of the ordinary. We joined him in the cab and chatted for hours. The Germans gradually disappeared. As time passed more Russian enlisted men arrived. From time to time the Soviet officer expressed doubts about the chief's arrival and I began to worry about Sergeant Warner, who had not returned.

At about 10:00 P.M., just as dusk approached and the lieutenant colonel's patience began to wane a USMLM car appeared out of the darkness. Maj. Dave Morgan, his driver, and Sergeant Warner all exited the vehicle. Sergeant Warner had been told to wait at the hotel for the car from Potsdam to arrive.

I told Major Morgan to get everything out of the burned hulk into the trunk of his vehicle. Majors Morgan and Clayborne and their drivers began the removal of everything they could find in the car. The Soviet officer approached me. "Where is your chief?"

"He's around. Wait, I'll get him."

In the dark surroundings there were now about fifty people wandering around the scene. I mingled in the crowd, shouting, "Chief! Chief!"

Major Clayborne found me in the darkness and told me that they had recovered everything from the car. He added, "The steel is so hard, the camera lenses are whole."

"Did you get two 400 mm lenses?"

"No, only one 400 mm lens."

"Look under my seat."

He returned. "We got it."

"So everything is out of the car."

"Nothing left but the ashes."

"Shovel the ashes into Morgan's trunk."

"You've got to be kidding!"

"No, I'm not kidding! Hurry. I've got to delay the Soviets."

The Soviet lieutenant colonel found me. "Where is your chief?"

"Gospodin, Colonel, he didn't come. He's in West Germany today."

"Who is going to make the decision?"

"I will."

Major Morgan gave me the signal that the car was clean. The Soviet was exasperated. "You could have done this twelve hours ago."

"No, I couldn't. I had no idea that our chief was in West Germany. You can take the car, but I would like it taken to the checkpoint at the Glienicke Bridge in Potsdam for transfer to us next Sunday at 1400 hours. If this is not satisfactory, please advise us during the week."

The lieutenant colonel's pleasant demeanor returned.

I asked, "How are you going to remove the car? Do you have a crane coming?"

"No, our fellows will lift it onto the truck."

Surprised to hear this, I said, "Your men can raise the car from the ground and put it onto a truck? I don't believe it."

"Watch us!"

The Soviet captain drove the flatbed truck beside the burned-out car. Soviet soldiers encircled the car and tried to lift it. Major Morgan's driver joined them. They actually got it off the ground on the first try.

I approached Major Morgan's driver and asked, "You're pushing down, aren't you?"

"No, Commander, I'm helping them."

I started to say, "Push down!" when I noticed the bloody hand of a Russian sergeant. That sight was enough to move me to help. I asked all of our people to assist in the effort, which I still thought was impossible. It wasn't. The car was lifted by manpower alone onto the truck.

I thanked the Soviet officers for their patience and wished all the soldiers the best. The five of us left for Potsdam. Exhausted, I slept most of the way. The Russians delivered the car to

Potsdam at 2:00 P.M. on the following Sunday. I had checked out the cameras and lenses from both the army and the air force. The steel lenses were so hard that the serial numbers were visible. I had the USMLM equipment custodian sign for their return.

During my two years in USMLM as a senior tour officer responsible for every reconnaissance trip, I had returned once with a severely damaged car and twice with a totally demolished car. It was time to go home!

24

Bye Bye, Commander Fahey

Several bizarre and unfortunate events related to my transfer from duty at the USMLM transpired from 27 February 1962 until I officially departed on 8 June. One serious breach of security led to a gratuitous intelligence dividend for the Soviet military. My detachment orders were signed by the chief of the navy's Bureau of Personnel, Rear Admiral W. R. Smedberg III, on 27 February and delivered to me on 5 March 1962. The bureau sent a copy of my orders to the USS *Thuban*, where I was to relieve the executive officer of the ship.

The orders simply read "When relieved detached duty Navy member, proceed port CONUS, thence proceed port in which USS *Thuban* (AKA-19) may be, arrival report CO duty XO." The orders were addressed to "CDR John A. Fahey, USN Military Liaison Mission to CINCGROUNDSUPP-FOR, Germany, Potsdam, Germany." This was the only address on the orders and it translated into a momentous mistake by the Bureau of Personnel. I received the orders by way of the commanding officer, Naval Support Activity–London. The copy produced for the USS *Thuban* was sent by the bureau directly to the ship.

Outside the intelligence field few military people were familiar with the existence of a unit of the American military assigned to the Soviet Army. Those on active duty in the U.S. Navy had even less knowledge of the liaison-spy organization than any other branch of service. My orders did not include any reference to "Soviet" in the strange acronym, CINCGROUNDSUPPFOR, even though eighteen months earlier the bureau's chief had authorized the wearing of a USMLM patch.

The USS *Thuban* officer, a naval academy graduate and submariner whom I was ordered to relieve as executive officer, decided to provide me with more information in advance than I had ever received before when reporting to a new command. In March 1962 he sent a large packet, containing biographies and personality profiles of all the ship's officers, the ship's characteristics, and the classified annual and quarterly operational schedules of all Atlantic Fleet ships (stamped "Confidential"). He addressed the huge bundle to me, care of the United States Military Liaison Mission to the commander in chief, Ground Support Forces, Potsdam, Germany.

USMLM had an army post office number in West Berlin. During the two years I served in the mission, the USMLM received only two mailings addressed to Potsdam: one, a newly developed army sniper scope that was sent to aid us in night observations of intelligence targets, arrived at the Potsdam Mission House a month late in a dirty and tattered box, after obviously being handled and closely scrutinized by the Russians and Germans; the other was the packet sent to me by the USS *Thuban*'s executive officer.

In the spring I had wondered about the sources the Stasi agents were using for getting information. The Soviet Army knew nothing about my forthcoming detachment from the USMLM, but the occupants of a tail car, the first that I had seen in more than a year, had driven abreast of me while its occupants waved and said, "Bye bye, Commander Fahey." In May I found out how the Stasi agents knew about my transfer as soon as I did.

A threadbare and torn package, postmarked in early March, arrived at the Potsdam House. The air force duty officer reviewed its contents. He was shocked to find classified material inside. He drove to Berlin and found me in the mission building.

"Commander, I want to turn this over to you before the army finds out about it. Obviously it was opened by the communists and it contains classified information."

I thanked him and inspected the package's contents, which were wrinkled and grimy from being repeatedly handled. The personality profiles of the USS *Thuban*'s officers listed each officer's strengths and weaknesses. The future scheduled dispositions of all Atlantic Fleet ships until 31 December 1962 had been compromised. There was more detailed information about the plans of the ships under the command of the commander in chief, U.S. Navy Amphibious Force–Atlantic. I decided not to inform the USMLM chief but instead to give the package to the representative in Germany of the commander in chief, U.S. Navy Forces–Europe.

While the executive officer of the USS *Thuban* violated approved security procedures, the Bureau of Personnel also was remiss in not using an APO address. The failure to do so caused the material to be sent directly into the hands of the Soviet Army.

After the fact I did not hear a single word about this unfortunate snafu. When I reported aboard *Thuban* the executive officer said, "How was I to know that you were attached to the Soviet Army? I thought that you were assigned to some ground support unit in West Germany."

The commander's reading of the copy of the orders would have been similar to the understanding of any of his contemporaries during the cold war. None would have imagined that one of their own had been given a "license to spy" behind the Iron Curtain. Even the chief of the navy's Bureau of Personnel did not seem to know that I was assigned to duty with the Soviet Army or that Potsdam was in East Germany.

Both the bureau and the commander had made this piece of intelligence collection easy for the communists. It was no wonder the Stasi had wide smiles on their faces when they hollered, "Bye Bye, Commander Fahey!"

25

Collection—The Bottom Line

Regardless of the number of detentions we endured, the subtle or dashing methods we used to lose tails, or the successes or failures we experienced during a multitude of liaison encounters, the United States Military Liaison Mission to the Group of Soviet Forces–Germany prevailed primarily because of the quantity and quality of the mission's intelligence collection. Regardless of the performance evaluations that USMLM members received in periodic army efficiency, air force effectiveness, and navy fitness reports, the bottom line in judging the merit of the contributions of a USMLM member was the intelligence results.

The presence of a naval officer as a gatherer of intelligence in the midst of the largest concentration of the opposition's ground and air forces during the cold war was an anomaly. The Huebner-Malinin Agreement specified that both the Soviet and American missions "consist of representatives of aviation, navy, and army." The missions' compositions may have suited the original intention of the agreement to establish liaison between the two armed forces, but cold war relationships soon changed the actual primary activity to one of intelligence collection. The predominance of army targets in the Soviet Zone transposed the one naval member at the mission into an intelligence agent for U.S. Army–Europe.

As the end of my USMLM assignment neared, I was concerned that an effort might be made to eliminate the navy billet at the mission. With the impending transfer of Lieutenant Colonel Fitzgerald, the chief had asked me to extend my tour of duty to become the deputy chief, mainly because of my Russian language ability and his favorable view of the way I handled detentions. He informed me that he was impressed with my knack of gracefully getting out of tight spots with the Soviets and he believed the Soviets did not intensely dislike me. After the Wall was erected he listened carefully to all of my ideas and adopted some of them as his own. The colonel told me that some of my suggestions were useful in his discussions with President Kennedy's envoy to Berlin, Gen. Lucius Clay.

In his letter requesting me as his deputy the chief needed to indicate my willingness to extend my tour of duty. He was not overjoyed when I declined. None of his expressed reasons for wanting me to extend my tour included my intelligence collection activities. At that moment it occurred to me that none of us, including the chief, had any idea how much or how good our individual reconnaissance production in the Soviet Zone was. Having heard veiled threats about a "need to change the air force team component, I knew that the naval billet at the USMLM might be seen as a weak link in the critical intelligence reporting arm of the mission.

In comparison with the British and French agreements with the Soviets, the Huebner-Malinin Agreement between the United States and the Soviet Union had only a small number of accredited personnel who could operate in the Soviet Zone. The USMLM was limited to a total of fourteen officers and enlisted men combined, while the British mission authorized eleven officers plus twenty technicians and other personnel; the French agreement authorized six officers plus twelve assistants. The U.S.S.R.-American agreement was the only one that authorized a navy representative, which would seem to protect the status of naval representation at the mission, but the U.S.-Soviet agreement also was the only one that permitted a change or amplification by mutual consent. Although I had declined to extend my tour of duty to be the USMLM deputy, I felt a strong obligation to ensure continuation of the navy billet there. The strongest case for maintaining a naval member's future presence in the mission would demonstrate that he or she contributed significantly to USMLM's collection of intelligence.

Like all the other tour officers I submitted army intelligence reports to the intelligence office of the U.S. Army–Europe in Heidelberg, West Germany. I sent my naval intelligence reports directly to the Office of Naval Intelligence in Washington. I gave any air intelligence information gathered or photographs taken to the USMLM air team.

I was aware that superiors at U.S. Army–Europe intelligence had commented favorably on a number of my reports, but I didn't have a record of how many intelligence reports I had submitted or how my reports stacked up against those of other USMLM tour officers. The only source available to retrieve this information was the USMLM operations office. I had a good relationship with the enlisted staff of the operations office and never complained about how my reports were processed.

Tours officers wrote their reports in longhand then gave them to the staff, who in turn typed and submitted them. The completed reports were not returned to the originators for proofreading. The British Military Liaison Mission was privy to all USMLM intelligence reports. On one occasion British headquarters questioned the site location noted on one of my army reports. The site was actually located one kilometer south of the reported location because my typed stencil report contained the digit five instead of the digit six in the six-digit coordinate system. The error was made in the typing, but after the

British complaint I made the correction and assumed the blame for the mistake. The enlisted men in the office were grateful that I stepped forward before they suffered for the error. I decided to ask Becker, a soldier in operations, to provide me with information on my reporting during the 1961 calendar year. "I would like to have a count of the total number of USMLM Intelligence reports sent to the commander in chief, U.S. Army–Europe, a count of the number that I submitted, and a tabulation of the evaluations received back from commander in chief, U.S. Army–Europe on my reports."

"Commander, I'll get yours but I shouldn't give you evaluations of others."

"All I want are the evaluations of my reports, but also the total number in each category of usability."

"I am willing to do that, but U.S. Army–Europe stopped sending evaluations after May 1961, although a couple were returned to us in October."

"Okay. I don't want to see information on any reports by other officers, nor evaluations of their reports."

Becker's research revealed the following: During 1961, USMLM sent 731 intelligence reports to U.S. Army–Europe. The naval member submitted 103 (14 percent) of these reports. A breakdown of the usability of evaluated naval member reports by U.S. Army–Europe for the first five months of 1961 follows:

Outstanding or Considerable Value—Over 20 percent
Contributive—Over 27 percent
Marginal—8 percent
Not Usable—0 percent

USMLM received only two evaluations after 31 May 1961. Usability of both reports was of considerable value. Evaluation of one of these reports, no. RG 499-61, submitted by the naval member follows:

> RG-499 Usability—Considerable value
>
> a. Reporting of the Type VI tower at Rostock is of vast importance to USAREUR analysts. Previous information has caused analysts to remove Rostock from tower location as it was reported that SED Haus was to be used as relay station.
>
> b. The reporting of the parabolas on SED houses is important to the analyst as it confirms the estimates made at U.S. Army–Europe.
>
> c. This was a fine job of reporting and filled some of the many gaps in this system."

In addition to graduating from the U.S. Naval Postgraduate School in Intelligence, my completion of other navy schools provided a good foundation for observing and reporting on Soviet Army units. The exposure to chemical and biological warfare in the navy's Damage Control School enabled me to recognize from a considerable distance a mobile military decontamination convoy on one of my first reconnaissance tours. No one else in USMLM had seen one before that time. By keeping alert for a close observation in the same area I was able to sight a second one early in 1961. I had a close look at a convoy with sixteen decontamination chambers. A truck with slurry trailed the mobile chambers. U.S. Army–Europe evaluated the sighting thus: "RG 009-61 Usability—Contributive. The validity rating expressed above represents U.S. Army–Europe agreement with the comments of the originator in para 6 of subject report. The unit to which the reported equipment belongs cannot be identified by U.S. Army–Europe although it is probably a decontamination platoon from a division chemical company. The alertness of the reporting officer to CBR activities is appreciated."

The first disappointment I experienced in my collection effort was rectified with photography. My father and one brother were accomplished artists. I had been trained in advanced engineering drawing and was accepted for a position as a U.S. government draftsman before I decided to join the navy. But I was never able to sketch freehand. On one of my first reconnaissance ventures I saw an armored personnel carrier unfamiliar to me. When I tried to draw a sketch of it after returning to Berlin, my USMLM colleagues laughed, convinced that the vehicle was a figment of my naval imagination. After that experience I photographed everything that moved in the Soviet Zone.

Evaluations of my reports always praised my photography, as these reports confirm:

> RG 111-61 Usability—Outstanding. This is the first information that we have received concerning existence of this site. Photos confirm existence of site. Any further information would be of value.
>
> RG 113-61 Usability—Contributive. Radio set is identified as R-104-MII. Photography of this type is of vast importance to the technical analyst. Continued effort should be continued to photograph the various radio sets in vehicles when possible.
>
> RG 180-61 Usability—Contributive. The BIG BAR with two END BOXES and a WITCH FOUR has been reported at this location several times. This is the only location at which a radar with two END BOXES has been reported. The photographs prove to be of definite value. Any additional information is desired.
>
> RG 177-61 Usability—Contributive. All equipment reported previously. Excellent photographs."

In addition to getting good photographs, many times taken under difficult conditions, the first identifications of sites, equipment, and specialized military units were of value. Many reports at the contributive level were similar to RG 176-61:

"RG 176-61 Usability—Contributive. These are the first confirmed orientation of the paraboloids on the Type III tower located at PG 58 5846 we have received."

Many times evaluators made favorable comments of my preparation of the report, similar to those noted in RG 267-61: "RG 267-61 Usability—1 (Considerable value—Outstanding). This is an excellent report and shows a great deal of thought and effort went into its production. Reports such as this one are of great value to the organizational analyst. Further reports of this nature are desired."

While I traveled almost exclusively on army reconnaissance tours, since the USMLM was dominated by army operational control, the army showed no interest in intelligence outside of specific U.S. Army priorities. It was extremely difficult at times for me to make trips to the northern coast. The U.S., British, and French military liaison missions divided the zone into three areas and each mission rotated weekly in assigned areas in order not to overlap coverage. This practice made the northern area available to me only every third week.

During the first week of October 1961 the northern sector was assigned to the USMLM, but the Soviets issued a temporary restrictions map and all mission cars and army drivers were engaged in covering the autobahns. Air Force Maj. Matt Warren offered me a driver for a three-day trip to the north. The USMLM operations officer was reluctant to permit the trip, but finally relented after limiting the tour to two days and requiring me to check all Soviet Army installations and the entire perimeters of the two northern restricted areas. This workload allowed only a quick pass by areas of naval interest.

Using my best persuasive abilities during the calendar year 1961 I managed to conduct fifteen reconnaissance trips to the Baltic Sea coastal area. As a result of these visits to northern East Germany I sent eighty intelligence reports to the Office of Naval Intelligence in Washington.

The 183 intelligence reports that I submitted to the U.S. Army and U.S. Navy far exceeded the number contributed during 1961 by any other USMLM members. During the year I was on "pass" status, which permitted entry into the Soviet Zone for nine-and-a-half months. During the rest of the year I was hospitalized and undergoing therapy after being injured in the mission car accident with Air Force Lieutenant Nick Yankowsky.

Liaison activities alone would not assure continuation of the naval member billet at the USMLM. Intelligence collection was the "bottom line" used in judging the merit of keeping a non–army or air force person in the Soviet Zone occupied by twenty-two Soviet divisions. I believe that four factors were paramount in permitting me, as a naval officer, to collect intelligence of army interest on a par with my fellow army officers.

1. Language Ability. The only other fluent Russian speaker was Lieutenant Colonel Fitzgerald. When I wore the navy uniform the Soviets believed that I was a communist military colleague and were apt to make disclosures to me that others weren't privy to.
2. Training. In addition to completing a postgraduate course in intelligence and obtaining an undergraduate degree in military science, in navy schools I was exposed to a wealth of information that gave me a broad background relative to Soviet operations.
3. Photography. I was unquestionably the most prolific photographer at the mission. Nothing escaped my camera lens. I continued my photography after retirement, including entering some private art shows and exhibits. My ability to capture waterfowl and other birds in flight was directly related to my earlier experiences in East Germany that demanded quickly taken but good quality photographs of military equipment on the ground or in the air.

4. Mnemonics. Everything seen in East Germany was remembered. No notes required. In addition to maps and cameras seized by the Stasi when they broke into an East German hotel room before my arrival, they also commandeered the mission officers' notes. I vowed then and there not to take notes or write during my forays for collection. A course in mnemonics was taught in 1953 at the U.S. Naval Intelligence School when I was a student by an expert on memory who served on the school's staff. Before arriving at the USMLM I used memory techniques only for fun. I would give demonstrations memorizing every page of a magazine, birth dates, telephone numbers, and the like. A year later, when unable to fly at Pensacola during bad weather, I entertained flight students by sitting around the hangar and memorizing within three minutes the order of an entire shuffled deck of cards. Three years later on the naval intelligence staff I taught the course on mnemonics. In the Soviet Zone I had ten thousand pigeon holes in my memory bank to store anything seen on a Soviet desk, numbers on Soviet military vehicles, license plate numbers, and even serial numbers inside tank engines and on other equipment. An agile memory was one of the most valuable assets for an intelligence collector.

I made known the results of Becker's research of my own collection effort and submitted a strong recommendation that a marine officer fulfill the USMLM Naval Member billet in the future. Along with the U.S. Army, the U.S. Marine Corps would derive the most benefit from information about a potential enemy's ground and air forces. A marine officer also would be better trained to face the rigors of ground reconnaissance duty. The close association of the U.S. Marine Corps with the U.S. Navy in the endeavor would satisfy the legality of the officer being the naval member of the mission, as specified in the Huebner-Malinin Agreement.

After the conclusion of my tour of duty, for the next twenty-eight years of USMLM's existence a marine officer was assigned as the naval member at the USMLM. I was the last naval officer in USMLM history to possess a "license to spy."

26

Anchors Aweigh

My departure from the USMLM and Berlin was not easy or routine. I had to turn in all army uniforms, while my navy uniforms had been destroyed during the last reconnaissance trip in the "fireball" vehicle. Entry into the Berlin command headquarters was necessary to arrange shipping of my household effects. Twice I was refused entry because I was in civilian clothes. Showing my active duty identification card didn't help because the security guards at the gate refused to recognize the entry "CDR" as a valid military rank. Finally when I did succeed in passing the gate security I decided to get a haircut in the command's barbershop. Fortunately General Watson was seated in the adjacent chair. The general was embarrassed by my tale of woe and paved the way for future visits by notifying the base security detachment that I was a naval officer and even in civilian clothes I should be admitted inside the base.

In honor of a detached member's departure it was a USMLM tradition for all USMLM personnel in Berlin to meet at the train station for the member and his family's send-off. On 8 June 1962 I was the only former member departing on the night army train to Frankfurt, West Germany. All of us at the station were surprised to see the Berlin army band present and playing a series of spirited marches. Barbara and I had attended many farewell ceremonies at the railroad station for our former USMLM colleagues, but had never witnessed the presence of an army band.

We said our good-byes. The USMLM chief gave me a letter which he asked me not to read until the train departed. He also told me that he had a final surprise for us. As soon as the train nudged forward the band began playing "Anchors Aweigh." The march continued as the train gathered speed. We could still hear the strains of the navy song until the music faded in the distance. That was the colonel's surprise. But another very unhappy colonel was aboard the train with us. Colonel Dean, as commander of Berlin's fighting force, already had endured numerous tensions brought on by the Wall's erection. When he sent his battle group to the Wall to assist the televising of a Jack Paar Show, not knowing what was going on, East Germany brought its army troops to the other side of the Wall to counter any possible offensive action by the Americans. Reprimands for this faux pas by the battle group were the result, though later they were rescinded. The band was at the train station to play for Colonel Dean's farewell because he had been relieved as a Berlin battle group commander. Riding off into the sunset to the strains of "Anchors Aweigh" was not a happy occasion for Colonel Dean. For the army band to play that march as the train left the station was his final indignity. I'm sure to him it was a reminder of one of the pranks the navy midshipmen played on his West Point classmates at the Army-Navy game.

Colonel Dean couldn't find anybody in a naval uniform on the train, because I was the only navy person aboard and I was in civilian clothes. I would, however, give him a 4.0, the highest navy mark, for trying to discover which navy person was responsible for the playing of the navy song by the army band, the band that was supposed to be there for his festive farewell to Berlin.

The chief's letter praised me as his "ace in the hole" with accomplishments second to none, recognition that I truly appreciated. But I must admit that I relished most of all the chief's parting gift to me—allowing me to hear "Anchors Aweigh" as my train departed.

Epilogue

Upon completion of his duty as an American liaison officer to the Soviet Army in East Germany, Commander John Fahey was recommended for a Legion of Merit and awarded the Army Commendation Medal for performing difficult liaison and operational duties and displaying diplomacy, perseverance, and great stamina while serving behind the Iron Curtain under conditions involving danger to life and limb.

During the year following his assignment as a navy officer with a "license to spy" behind the Iron Curtain, Commander Fahey served as executive officer of the USS *Thuban*. At sea as the U-2 incident developed, sightings of Soviet merchant ships en route to Cuba provided him with opportunities to again photograph Soviet Army equipment and initiate intelligence reports. His retirement from active military service almost a year later (1963) was a departure from spying and intelligence collection, but the change permitted him to continue to employ his Russian language and leadership abilities in civilian life.

Upon retirement his title changed from Commander Fahey to Professor Fahey and he served as an educator of the Russian language for twenty-five years. He was retired in 1988 as an associate professor emeritus at Old Dominion University. Professor

Fahey led numerous study tours to the U.S.S.R., studied in a Moscow State University program, and conducted a site visit of the new U.S. Embassy in Moscow for an American contractor.

He served three years as president of the Virginia chapter of the American Association of Teachers of Slavic and East European Languages, two years as president of the Virginia Foreign Language Association, nine years as a member of the Virginia Beach Public School Board, three years as chairman of the board of directors and executive committee of the Hampton Roads Educational Telecommunications Association (WHRO-TV, WHRO-FM, and WHRV-FM), president of the Virginia Beach Rotary Club, governor of Rotary International District 7600 (central and southeastern Virginia), secretary and treasurer of the Virginia Beach unit of the American Cancer Society, president of AARP Chapter 4643, and two years as president of the Naval Airship Association. He serves currently on the Virginia Beach Mayor's Commission on Aging and as president of Old Dominion University's Institute for Learning in Retirement.

His teaching at Old Dominion University has been recognized in several awards: 1974 Delta Phi Omega Distinguished Faculty Award; the 1980 Robert L. Stern Award for Outstanding Teacher in the College of Arts and Letters; the 1982 Alan Rufus Tonelson Distinguished Faculty Award; and the Delta Sigma Lambda Alumnae 2000 "Most Favorite Professor" Award. The Virginia Beach Education Association awarded Professor Fahey its 1990 Academic Freedom and Educational Excellence Award.

John Fahey has authored three books, and his articles have appeared in *Missiles and Rockets*, *Space Journal*, the *Russian Review*, the *Russian Language Journal*, *U.S. Naval Institute Proceedings*, *Officer Review*, and *Torch*. He lives in Virginia Beach with Barbara, his wife of fifty-six years.

Appendix
Huebner-Malinin Agreement

Military Liaison Missions Accredited to the Soviet and United States Commanders in Chief of the Zones of Occupation Germany

In conformity with the provisions of Article 2 of the Agreement on "Control Mechanism in Germany," November 14, 1944, the US and the Soviet Commanders-in-Chief of the Zones of Occupation in Germany have agreed to exchange Military Liaison Missions accredited to their staffs in the zones and approve the following regulations concerning these missions:

1. These missions are military missions and have no authority over quadri-partite military government missions or purely military government missions of each respective country, either temporarily or permanently, on duty in either zone. However, they will render whatever aid or assistance to said military government missions as is practicable.
2. Missions will be composed of air, navy, and army representatives. There will be no political representatives.
3. The missions will consist of not to exceed fourteen (14) officers and enlisted personnel. This number will include all necessary technical personnel, office clerks, personnel with

special qualifications, and personnel required to operate radio stations.

4. Each mission will be under the orders of a senior member of the mission who will be appointed and known as "Chief of the United States (or Soviet) Military Mission."
5. The Chief of the Mission will be accredited to the Commander-in-Chief of the occupation forces. In the United States Zone the mission will be accredited to Commander-in-Chief, United States European Command. In the Soviet Zone the mission will be accredited to the Commander-in-Chief of the Group of Soviet Occupational Forces in Germany.
6. In the United States Zone the Soviet Mission will be offered quarters in the region of Frankfurt.
7. In the Soviet Zone the United States Mission will be offered quarters at or near Potsdam.
8. In the United States Zone the Chief of the Soviet Mission will communicate with A/C of Staff, G-3, United States European Command.
9. In the Soviet Zone the Chief of the United States Mission will communicate with the Senior Officer of the Staff of Commander-in-Chief.
10. Each member of the missions will be given identical travel facilities to include identical permanent passes in Russian and English languages permitting complete freedom of travel wherever and whenever it will be desired over territory and roads in both zones, except places of disposition of military units, without escort or supervision. Each time any member of the Soviet or United States mission wants to visit United States or Soviet headquarters, military government offices, forces, units, military schools, factories, and enterprises which are under United States or Soviet control, a corresponding request must be made to Director, Op-

erations, Plans, Organization and Training, European Command, or Senior Officer, Headquarters, Group of Soviet Occupational Forces in Germany. Such requests must be acted upon within 24–72 hours. Members of the missions are permitted allied guests at the headquarters of respective missions.

11. a. Each mission will have its own radio station for communications with its own headquarters.
    b. In each case couriers and messengers will be given facilities for free travel between the headquarters of the mission and headquarters of their respective Commander-in-Chief. These couriers will enjoy the same immunity which is extended to diplomatic couriers.
    c. Each mission will be given facilities for telephone communication through the local telephone exchange at the headquarters, and they also will be given facilities such as mail, telephone, telegraph through the existing means of communication when the members of the mission will be traveling within the zone. In case of a breakdown in the radio installation, the zone commanders will render all possible aid and will permit temporary use of their own systems of communication.
12. The necessary rations. P. O. L. supplies and household services for the military missions will be provided for by the headquarters to which accredited, by method of mutual compensation in kind, supplemented by such items as desired to be furnished by their own headquarters. In addition the respective missions or individual members to the missions may purchase items of Soviet or United States origin which must be paid for in currency specified by the headquarters controlling zone where the purchase is made.
13. The buildings of each mission will enjoy full right of extraterritoriality.

14. a. The task of the mission will be to maintain liaison between both Commanders-in-Chief and their staffs.
    b. In each zone the mission will have the right to engage in matters of protecting the interests of their nationals and to make representations accordingly as well as in matters of protecting their property interests in the zone where they are located. They have the right to render aid to people of their own country who are visiting the zone where they are accredited.
15. This agreement may be changed or amplified by mutual consent to cover new subjects when the need arises.
16. This agreement is written in Russian and English languages and both texts are authentic.
17. This agreement becomes valid when signed by Deputy Commanders of United States and Soviet Zones of Occupation.

C. R. Huebner

Lieutenant-General HUEBNER	Colonel-General MALININ
Deputy Commander-in-Chief European Command Forces	Deputy Commander-in-Chief Chief of Staff of the Group of Soviet Occupation Forces in Germany

Note: The original English copy of this agreement on file in SGS, U.S. Army–Europe, shows that it was signed 5 April 1947 by Huebner and Malinin.

Index

About the Author

Cdr. John Fahey served for twenty years in the U.S. Navy as a combat airship command pilot during World War II, operations officer and executive officer at sea, and in various naval intelligence assignments. After retiring from the navy in 1963, Fahey began a second career as an educator. He taught for twenty-five years, twenty-two at Old Dominion University, where he won awards as the College of Arts and Letters most outstanding teacher and the university's most distinguished faculty member. Along with his teaching career, Commander Fahey has served as president of many educational and community organizations, Governor of District 7600, Rotary International, president of the Naval Airship Association, and chairman of the board of directors for Hampton Roads Educational Telecommunications Association (WHRO-TV, WHRO-FM, and WHRV-FM). He has also written two books, *A Cartoon View of Russia* and *Wasn't I the Lucky One*, and over thirty of his articles have been published in such scholarly and professional journals as *Missiles and Rockets*, *Space Journal*, U.S. Naval Institute *Proceedings*, *The Russian Review*, *Russian Language Journal*, *Conservative Digest*, and *The Torch*. Commander Fahey lives in Virginia Beach, Virginia, with his wife, Barbara.

The Naval Institute Press is the book-publishing arm of the U.S. Naval Institute, a private, nonprofit, membership society for sea service professionals and others who share an interest in naval and maritime affairs. Established in 1873 at the U.S. Naval Academy in Annapolis, Maryland, where its offices remain today, the Naval Institute has members worldwide.

Members of the Naval Institute support the education programs of the society and receive the influential monthly magazine *Proceedings* and discounts on fine nautical prints and on ship and aircraft photos. They also have access to the transcripts of the Institute's Oral History Program and get discounted admission to any of the Institute-sponsored seminars offered around the country.

The Naval Institute also publishes *Naval History* magazine. This colorful bimonthly is filled with entertaining and thought-provoking articles, first-person reminiscences, and dramatic art and photography. Members receive a discount on *Naval History* subscriptions.

The Naval Institute's book-publishing program, begun in 1898 with basic guides to naval practices, has broadened its scope to include books of more general interest. Now the Naval Institute Press publishes about one hundred titles each year, ranging from how-to books on boating and navigation to battle histories, biographies, ship and aircraft guides, and novels. Institute members receive significant discounts on the Press's more than eight hundred books in print.

Full-time students are eligible for special half-price membership rates. Life memberships are also available.

For a free catalog describing Naval Institute Press books currently available, and for further information about subscribing to *Naval History* magazine or about joining the U.S. Naval Institute, please write to:

Membership Department
U.S. Naval Institute
291 Wood Road
Annapolis, MD 21402-5034
Telephone: (800) 233-8764
Fax: (410) 269-7940
Web address: www.navalinstitute.org